Father Robinson, private secretary to Paul-Emile Cardinal Léger until the latter's retirement, is Chairman of the Department of Philosophy at Marianopolis College, and part-time lecturer in philosophy at McGill University. He holds the Ph.D. degree from Edinburgh.

FAITH AND REFORM

FAITH *and* REFORM

A Reinterpretation
of *Aggiornamento*

edited by
Jonathan Robinson

New York

Fordham University Press

1969

Acknowledgments

To Darton, Longman & Todd, Ltd., London, and Helicon Press, Inc., Baltimore, for Karl Rahner, *Theological Investigations.*

To Faber & Faber, Ltd., London, and Harcourt, Brace & World, Inc., New York, for T. S. Eliot, *Collected Poems, 1909–1962.*

To Faber & Faber, Ltd., London, and Random House, Inc., New York, for W. H. Auden, *For the Time Being*, copyright © 1946 by W. H. Auden.

To A. D. Peters & Co., London, for Boris Pasternak, *In the Interlude: Poems, 1945–1960*, translated by Henry Kamen. Reprinted by permission of A. D. Peters & Co.

To Pontifical Institute of Mediaeval Studies, Toronto, for *Theology of Renewal.*

To University of Notre Dame Press for John H. Miller, ed., *Vatican II: An Interfaith Appraisal.*

To Western Publishing Co., Inc., Racine, Wisconsin, for excerpts from the Decrees of the Ecumenical Council, taken from *The Documents of Vatican II*, published by Western Publishing Co., Inc., The America Press, and Association Press; copyright © 1966 by The America Press. Used by permission.

Contents

FAITH AND REFORM

Editor's Preface

THIS BOOK IS A SELECTION from a series of papers which had as their common theme the faith in the world today. The papers were given at Marianopolis College, Montreal, during the winter of 1968. The college, although not affiliated with McGill University, is located in the centre of the McGill campus, and serves, in cooperation with the Newman Club, as a centre for Catholic activities on the campus. It was in the spirit of the Newman apostolate that these lectures were planned, and they were intended, under the inspiration of the great cardinal, to be scholarly and yet relevant to the needs of their hearers.

It has become a commonplace today to read that the educated laity is finding it harder and harder to identify with the Church, either as they find it in their local community or at the national and international level. It is possible, perhaps, to attribute some of this malaise to the universal human temptation to grumble, as well as to the activities of people who seem to make a profession of negative and unhelpful criticism. Again, it may be, notwithstanding professions to the contrary, that many people are looking for guidance in new and unfamiliar situations and resent the fact that they are not finding it. Yet when these and similar allowances are made, it seems evident that the active mistrust or indifference between what is called nowadays the official Church and the rest of the people of God is one of the more frightening marks of our time.

There are those who would lay all the blame for this situation at the door of the hierarchy. The cynical observation of Machiavelli[1] that ecclesiastical principalities are acquired either by ability or good luck but are maintained with neither, can be found repeated in substance, if with less elegance of form, in any number of religious newspapers and weeklies. Criticism does not in itself show that things are in a bad way: it may be a sign of life and vitality, and, as Cardinal Léger was fond of pointing out, some critics are impelled by a love of the Church to try to improve the situation in which they find themselves. On the other hand, there is a whole range of criticism which is based on naturalistic and rationalistic categories which leave no room for the divine element in the Church, and which at its most extreme seems to identify the divine with man's striving after the good. God the creator, the incarnation, sin and grace, revelation and the last things are not so much denied as left out of the centre of the picture. If all these elements are forgotten, and some kind of evolutionary, self-developing *je ne sais quoi* is put in their place, it is no wonder that the

Church and churchmen are under constant attack. Once we lose sight of the fact that the Church is the mystery of the abiding presence on earth of the mercy of Christ, and begin to judge her in purely earthly terms, it does not require genius to conclude that there are more efficient ways of organizing social work, fighting for human rights, or celebrating big ceremonies.

It was precisely because it was felt that this supernatural element of the faith is not being sufficiently stressed today that this series of studies was originally planned. Those presenting them are united in the view that a discussion of the sort of problems which do in fact face people living in the world when they want to think about the central issues of their faith is very much in order. A great many of the most conscientious and concerned laity live with a kind of uneasy sense that in some way or other Catholic Christianity has been shown to be, if not false, at least somehow doubtful. Once this attitude prevails—and it is one which is more widespread than some seem to imagine —then people become bored and indifferent, or else hostile and bitter, towards and with the Church.

None of us imagines that it is enough to write papers in order to correct this situation. On the other hand, it does not follow from this that discussion and attempts to emphasize what has been overlooked are a waste of time. Presumably educated people read books, and if it is the educated laity who are finding things difficult just now we may hope some of them will read this book.

These studies, then, are an effort to emphasize certain aspects of the faith which seem to be overlooked in popular writing about the Church, and particularly about the Second Vatican Council. The Church's efforts to unload the useless baggage accumulated in its journey through the centuries is only the negative side of *aggiornamento*. The positive basis for this critical —some have thought it iconoclastic and destructive— work of the council was the belief that nothing is more important to the Church than her task of proclaiming the Gospel to all mankind, and her mission of sanctifying her children through the sacramental and liturgical life of the mystical body. It is precisely with these positive aspects of *aggiornamento* that the writers of this book are concerned, and we have no desire to take part in some sort of crusade. Where it seems to us that important parts of the faith have been overlooked, or played down in the interest of what we think are false concessions to the spirit of the age or because of confused thinking, we have not hesitated to say so. But we do not think that the best way of dealing with error, at least on the part of individuals, is to issue anathemas and condemnations, for we hold, in the spirit of Pope Paul VI's encyclical *Ecclesiam suam*, that dialogue, understood as a real exchange of views and not as the complimentary interchange of vapid trivialities which so often pass as a substitute for it, is the way in which truth is best safeguarded. "It is a miserable time," as Newman said, "when a man's Catholic profession is no voucher for his orthodoxy, and when a teacher of religion may be within the Church's pale, yet external to her faith." [2] This is true, and probably describes our own time, but in refusing to allow real debate and by demanding the intervention of authority at every point we show a lack of confidence in the truth which in time will make its own way, strengthened and deepened by its contest with error and by its effort to understand what merit there is in positions incompatible with the faith. We are, however, to repeat: more interested with emphasizing some of the central Christian affirmations, than in looking for error.

With these general remarks in mind we can now go on to outline the argument of the papers. The first of these lays the groundwork and provides the frame of reference for the subsequent studies by emphasizing certain basic notions of the Catholic point of view. The doctrine that Christianity is a revelation committed to the Church is underlined, and from this the consequence is drawn that Catholicism is of necessity an historical religion, and that the faith is, in the words of Newman, "social . . . dogmatic, and intended for all ages." [3]

The next tripartite paper, by Fr. Irwin, is concerned with the interpretation of the New Testament today. It is in the New Testament that the faith is first found written down and guaranteed by God's authority. There can be little doubt that one of the less happy byproducts of the revival of Biblical studies has been an increase in an agnostic or skeptical view towards Scripture. This may have been a price which had to be paid for all the benefits which a return to the sources has brought. On the other hand, merely because a point of view is widespread is not an adequate reason for its being accepted, and in his paper Fr. Irwin argues that the proclamation of salvation which is central to Scripture is more closely related to history than to myth, and that this history is affirmed in the creeds which are proposed for our belief by the Church. The Church's role as an interpreter of Scripture is part of her legacy from the Apostles, and it is only through the New Testament as interpreted au-

thoritatively by the Church that we can find that unity
of faith for which St. Paul prayed when he asked the
Ephesians to maintain the unity of spirit in the bond
of peace.[4]

This unity of faith, however, was not intended
merely for the apostolic age, and in his study "Reformation and *Aggiornamento*" Fr. McConica takes up
the historical theme. He shows how the history of
the Church is itself revealing because it is the work
not only of man, but of God as well. We can never
learn what *sentire cum ecclesia* means without knowing history, and how the Church has responded to
different challenges and crises in the past. The author examines the revolutionary situation of the sixteenth century to see how the unique vitality of the
Church responds to new situations in order to adapt,
to conserve, and to grow. There are many parallels
between the time of the Reformation and our own.
Yet, while secularization, as well as the anti-sacra-
mental and anti-theological trends of our own day all
have their counterparts in the sixteenth century, there
is much that is new and hopeful in the present situation. The Church, which for the last four hundred
years has been in so many ways a synagogue in its
exclusiveness and intolerance, is returning to earlier
ways of thought and behaviour, and it is this which
makes the council and its effects so disturbing to a
great many people. But there is no room for the immobilism of despair, because the tremendous upheavals
and changes are themselves signs of the vitality of the
spirit working in Christ's body to ensure that the
Gospel is preached to man as he is in the twentieth
century.

In the last, two-part paper Dr. Suttor examines how

the traditional faith of the Church continues to be, as it has always been, a stumbling block and foolishness for those who do not believe. He has some biting comments to make on those who have tried to compromise the difficult aspects of Christianity in the interests of a false modernity, and he insists that the traditional Christian values and positions are as relevant today as they have ever been.

The message of the series can best be summed up by saying that the present situation is full of hope if we can maintain our faith in the great affirmations of Catholic Christianity and not capitulate to the spirit of the age which has no time for revelation or for the belief that the Church and her work are the continuation of our Lord's mission. But this is only half the battle; we must learn to go on with the work of *aggiornamento*, to revise structures and to be ruthless in rejecting what no longer serves the preaching of the Word or obscures the reality of Christ's abiding presence with us.

It is hard to be patient, and it requires faith, and discernment, and toughness of mind. What we are now witnessing is the curious internal dialectic by which the Church learns, suffers and progresses; only this time it is proceeding openly and not in secret and subterranean channels. It seems to me that we must expect provisional solutions while this internal dialectic proceeds. We should not be so stung by the tensions and embarrassments this causes that we render ourselves unable to appreciate what a striking testimony to the confidence and integrity of the modern Catholic Church this is. If we do not keep the positive elements uppermost in our mind we may find ourselves, in our apathy, the allies of a new and most subtle kind of immobilism, a stagnation of spirit, which

recalls the warning question about whether the Son of
Man, on His return, would find faith upon the earth.[5]

NOTES

1. Machiavelli, *The Prince*, Ch. 11. "It now only remains to
   us to speak of ecclesiastical principalities, with regard to
   which the difficulties lie wholly before they are possessed.
   They are acquired either by ability or by fortune; but are
   maintained without either, for they are sustained by ancient
   religious customs, which are so powerful and of such
   quality, that they keep their princes in power in whatever
   manner they proceed and live."
2. J. H. Newman, "A Form of Infidelity of the Day," in *The
   Idea of a University* (New York: Doubleday Image Books,
   1959), Sec. 2, No. 1.
3. J. H. Newman, *An Essay on the Development of Christian
   Doctrine* (London: Longmans, Green and Co., 1897), Ch.
   II, Sec. 2, No. 13. "If Christianity is both social and dogmatic, and intended for all ages, it must humanly speaking
   have an infallible expounder."
4. Ephesians 4:1–6.
5. From the concluding paragraph of Fr. McConica's paper.

I

Through Faith for Faith

Jonathan Robinson

St. Paul, writing to the Romans, said that the Gospel was the power of God for salvation to everyone who has faith, "for in it," he continues, "the righteousness of God is revealed through faith, for faith." [1] Through faith and for faith might very well be taken as the leading idea of these papers for they represent an attempt, from several standpoints, to deal with some of the problems which confront the believer in the world of today. These are problems which face the individual Christian who can no longer count on social pressures and observances to buttress up his faith, but who is subjected to a whole gamut of arguments, suasions, and subtle pressures to abandon faith. In so far as these papers deal with these arguments, as well as seeking to analyse and detect these

suasions and pressures, they may be said to be on behalf of faith, *for* faith.

Yet, it is only *through* faith, by meditating on some
of its implications in the face of a variety of questions
from history, Scripture, morality, epistemology, and
metaphysics that the believer will be able to face the
many pressures on his faith. And so while these studies
are for faith, they are intended, at least in the first
instance, for the believer. They are not exercises in
persuasion, in apologetics, but are a series of discus-
sions on the kind of problems which do in fact face
thoughtful people living in the world about some of
the central issues of their faith. Such people, with no
technical training in theology, do not live in an atmosphere of the acceptance of the basic verities of
Christianity; rather, they live in a world which is,
intellectually speaking, a kind of rag-bag of miscel-
laneous information gleaned from the newspapers and
other media, and especially from the "religious section" of the ubiquitous weeklies.

It is, then, for believers living in the modern world
that these papers are written, and more especially for
those who profess the faith of the Roman Church.
They represent an attempt to understand our own
position as Roman Catholics in a deeper and more
coherent way. They are not put forward in the interests of a narrow fanaticism, but so that we may become more aware of the riches of Christ which our
own tradition contains. We have to start from where
we are, and understand what we are, if we are to grow
towards other Christians, and unbelievers, in ways
which will foster true unity and understanding. Nothing will be gained in the long run, and much may be
lost, if we obscure the differences between the Church

and the world, or the differences which separate those who follow Christ.

The fundamental reason why we owe loyalty to our own denomination is that it is where the believer actually finds Christ. Christians love their churches because, when all is said and done, they recognize in their different ways that they testify and witness to the truth of Christ. A Christian recognizes that he personally is put into contact with the values of the Gospel and with Christ Himself by means of his Church, through that group of believers to which he belongs and where the word of God is proclaimed and the sacraments are administered. The Church is accepted because it is believed that although much could be changed for the better, nonetheless, in the final analysis, it is recognized that the Church is the bearer of the Evangelion, the good news. Therefore, what we need is a deeper loyalty to our tradition, and a strengthening of our grasp on the truths into which we come in contact through its agency.

This deepened loyalty is not to be understood in a narrow, hard or exclusive sense, but as a growing awareness of the treasures of Christ which the Church contains. Until we do this we will never be able to see what in fact we do not need to hold on to, what theological views can be discarded without disloyalty, and what must be tenaciously maintained. This is no easy business, but it is not enough to confess the name of Jesus in order to achieve unity with other Christians, or meet the problems of faith in the world today. It requires a courageous honesty to be a believer today, but that very honesty requires that we know ourselves.

Having said all this we are now faced with the obvious fact that it seems to be more difficult to say with precision what we mean when we talk about faith than it was a few years ago. A great many of the obvious sort of external marks of the Church seem to have been more or less quietly dropped, and the world of fasting and abstinence, first Fridays and Corpus Christi processions seems suddenly to have vanished. It is not always too clear what has been put in the place of these familiar landmarks, or where we should go when we become confused at their overthrow.

One place we do go is to the results of the work of the theologians, or at least we go to what we are told are the results of their work; but we are soon disappointed, for it is a commonplace to say that theologians and the rest of us live in very different worlds. One reaction to this fact is to try to deny to theologians their undoubted right to use technical language in the elaboration of their work, or else to discount the relevance of theology for our own lives. Often a third kind of position is opted for which is to concede that theology must be a technical discipline, but to depend on the popularizers, the people who write for the weekly magazines or newspapers, to tell us about theological developments, the significance of Vatican II, or the writings of the famous theologians.

This dependence on the work of others is not peculiar to theology. We are all at the mercy of experts. Whether we be lawyers or doctors or teachers, we are all dependent on the research and learning of those who are proficient in fields other than our own. This is even true within a particular discipline—the criminal lawyer will have to consult the corporation lawyer, the expert in pathology will require information from the chemist, and so on. We are still more dependent on those who summarize and paraphrase the developments of different disciplines; this is as true of theology and religion as of anything else. It also seems to be a fact, perhaps because we do live in a world which is so dependent on the learning of others, that we are also living in a world where private speculation about serious matters has become impossible. All of us know that the time when theology could be written and studied within a more or less restricted circle has passed. In spite of the fact that religion is supposed to be dying, there seems to be no lack of interest in ecclesiastical and theological matters. But there is a real problem here, as the possibility of speculation and dialogue about serious and controversial matters in private has become almost impossible, and a great many people have suffered from this fact.

When I say that many have suffered from the public sort of theology with which we are forced to live, I do not mean only those theologians who have had their perfectly legitimate speculations travestied by those seeking to make news; I also mean all the rest of us. Those who, wishing to be loyal to the Church, and welcoming the new developments of Vatican II, are at the same time perplexed and distressed by a great deal of what we are told at third or fourth hand, are the results of the new theology. The Mass has suddenly become a fraternal meal, the bodily resurrection of our Lord is pronounced to be an irrelevant matter, the idea of integrity or honesty seems to have replaced the fact that Catholicism has always insisted that it had something to do with the idea of truth. We are left with the impression that Scripture says very little, and what it does say is so obscure that only the expert can understand its hidden, real, and not very relevant meaning. Preaching and catechetics at times seem to have altered from the admittedly difficult task of preaching the word of God into seeing how much

Jones will swallow, and, in the words of Mgr. Knox, we have arrived at a time

> When suave politeness temp'ring bigot zeal
> Corrected "I believe" to "one does feel." [2]

All these impressions, or complaints, are not necessarily the bigot mouthings of disillusioned reaction; they are, on the contrary, the effect of the seepage from a great deal of the writing about the council. That people are confused cannot be denied. Some of this confusion may be a good thing if it encourages analysis and self-reliance, but all too often so much seems to be called into question that people do not even know where to begin. These papers are a modest attempt to deal with some of the problems before the public today, and all of them seek to show the continuity of the catholic tradition which, we are united in believing, is the only basis for a sound judgement on theology, and the Church in the world.

INTENDED FOR ALL AGES

The faith, Cardinal Newman wrote, is social, dogmatic, and intended for all ages.[3] The last of these characteristics explains in part what has been happening in the Church. The council called the Church the bride of Christ, the mystical body, the vineyard of the Lord, and the people of God, but to many generous hearts and open minds the Church had ceased to give a convincing enough account of herself for people to see her as the light shining in the darkness, as the sign and sacrament of the continuing love of God for His people. The Church, rather than appearing as the home for all mankind, seemed unfriendly, narrow, and restricting. The council was the Church's magnificent attempt to show that none of these impressions need be true. The effort to unload the irrelevant baggage of the centuries, and to bring the Church into closer contact with the living, moving centre of human affairs has been called *aggiornamento*.

The activity of the council with its efforts to make the Church and the faith more relevant to the modern world was not prompted by a desire to seek an accommodation with that world which would in any way betray the sacred trust of the Church. On the contrary, the activity of the council was undertaken so that the supreme task of proclaiming the Gospel to all the children of God, and the mission of sanctifying those children through the sacramental and liturgical life of the mystical body, might become more effective. If the Church is to realize this task she must in some sense be the contemporary of those to whom she addresses herself. If you are trying to tell people something, you must first of all have some idea of what you are trying to say, and secondly you have to know something about the people to whom you are speaking. When we are told that the council was not a dogmatic council, but rather pastoral in its character, part of what we are being told is that it is the second question which gave dimension and direction to the deliberations and documents of the bishops. What the bishops were concerned to emphasize was the *relevance* of the faith to the modern world, not *the faith* which is (in fact) relevant to the modern world.

In a very beautiful and profound essay on "Lumen Gentium and the Fathers"—that is, on the *Dogmatic Constitution on the Church* promulgated by the council, and its relation to the great post-apostolic leaders of the Church who are especially revered as witnesses to the Christian tradition—Fr. Henri de Lubac, s.j., has summed up the matter in the following way:

. . . there is less description of the mother than of the
children, less of the house than of those who dwell therein,
less of the voice summoning men to assemble in Christ
(*convocatio*) than of the results of the assembly (*con-
gregatio*). Nevertheless, we should notice that this is a
question only of proportion and nuance, and that between
these two aspects there is no yawning abyss.[4]

The Church at the council, then, concentrated on the
recipient of the message, the means by which it was
to be communicated, and the world to which the message was to be addressed. Nor, as the *Pastoral Constitution on the Church in the Modern World* shows,
was the Church afraid to show that she had much to
learn from this modern world. Surely all this is desirable, and showed the true character of the Church
which must always be missionary until all men are
gathered into her. Those who continually harped at
the scandal being done to the faith of the charcoal
burner were given short shrift, and it was made clear
that the bishops of the world were determined that
the riches of Christ should be shared with all mankind,
and not kept as a kind of sacred preserve for the rela-
tively small proportion of humanity who were in the
visible unity of the Church. There is, then, the emphasis on sharing the faith, and the world to which the
faith is to be preached.

Yet, if the message of the Church, the faith which
is intended for all ages, must be adapted, it follows if
words have any sense at all that there is *a* faith which
is being adapted, *a* message which men are trying to
make more relevant. So, in fact, we find the council
documents on both revelation and the Church stating
very clearly that the Christian faith is a revelation;
however we understand this word, it means at least
that there is something given, from God to man.

Christianity is not, therefore, some sort of philosophical construction or ideology. Revelation, to put it in its least question-begging way, puts us into contact with God and Christ in a way which is unique and final. Or, to speak even more simply in the language of St. John,[5] revelation teaches us the truth: the truth about God, Christ, man and the world, and the nature and destiny of creation; not *a* truth, or an insight, but *the* truth. Again this revelation is intimately connected with the Church, for it is to the Church that this revelation has been given. Says Father Schillebeeckx:

This, then, is the Council's central affirmation: religiousness receives its basic form, in accordance with God's will, in the Church of Christ. Christianity in its ecclesial form is objectively the mature appearance of all true religiousness . . . while frankly recognizing the religious values of all humanity, even as a "preparation for the Gospel," the Council clearly affirms, on the ground of the Church's faith in Christ, the redeemer, the absolute uniqueness of the Christian religion.[6]

No one can claim that Father Schillebeeckx is some sort of hidebound conservative insensitive to the needs of his time, and this brings me to an important point. The world of even the most radical of the Catholic theologians who helped make the council is a very different one from that presented to us by the mass media and the trivializers. One cannot read the works of the great theologians without being made intensely aware of the unique value they place on Christ and the Church. It is so much the air they breathe, and the force which sustains them, that they are enabled to speculate and advance hypotheses which, if taken in isolation from this atmosphere and explicit adherence to Christ and the Church, can be made to seem so strange and at times even offensive.

The climate of opinion in North America at the present time is such that it welcomes anything which can be interpreted as openness, encouragement of secular values, ecumenism, and generally the new look which the Church has tried to give herself. This climate is one which, de facto, has little interest in the vital point that Christianity claims to be a revelation, and that this revelation in the person of Christ and His continuing presence in the Church is the dynamic centre from which all else radiates and upon which everything else depends. If we put the new emphasis of Vatican II together with the understandable reluctance of the media to deal with what is perennial and supernatural we arrive at a situation which a great many people find confusing, and one in which it is difficult for them to keep their bearings. In this way the very desire to make the Gospel more accessible to all, and the wish to show that the faith is intended for all ages including our own, have in fact obscured for many the abiding certainties of Christ's revelation which it is the Church's business to proclaim.

SOCIAL

We cannot, however, ascribe all the blame—if that is the correct word—for the present confusion to the news media working on a public opinion which has no great interest in the claims of Christianity to be supernatural. There are as well a great many Catholics whose work has had the effect of obscuring the notion that the faith is a unique and final revelation committed to the Church. Newman, in saying that the faith was social and dogmatic, was insisting precisely on this point that Christianity is not merely a religion which concerned the individual's private, "interior" life; but it also has its social, community or institutional aspect, and that this institutional aspect is possible only in terms of a common belief.

To speak about community today is a difficult task, as it is often used in a very special way to mean some sort of spiritual association of like-minded people who are held together by no institutional ties. In this way community is a term of commendation, while institution—and all its variants—are words of reproach. "Institutional Christianity," "the institutional Church"— these, it is said, are the agencies which have smothered the true growth of the spirit. There is, of course, enough evidence in history and in the present day to enable us to sympathize with the motives of the people who speak, and presumably think, in this way; but it is one thing to appreciate a motive, and quite another to subscribe to a position which neither makes sense, nor can be readily made to square with the Church's solemn teaching about herself.

The position does not make much sense because it seeks on the one hand to make sincerity, or individual conviction, the basis for true community; but at the same time wishes to preserve a sort of sense of solidarity which can only be achieved by the pursuit of a common ideal. The view seems to be maintained that religion is personal and private, that it is concerned above all else with the individual's sincerity before God (or even, if he is very modern, with his sincerity —full stop), and yet this sincerity flows over into common action, and a common point of view. Those who share this activity and point of view are somehow or other members of a community which is not institutional.

Even if we prescind altogether from the embarrassing fact of sin, which, it would seem, history and experience have shown us we should not do; even forgetting sin, the position makes little sense, because, amongst a great many other reasons, it ignores the social nature of belief itself. This may be made clearer if we remember the interesting fact that this attitude towards the individual's role in the question of faith and community is only one example of a widespread movement in modern thought and of which we can see another instance in modern ethical writing which has concentrated almost exclusively on intention. The notion that moral philosophy is concerned with acts, with things done in the real world, is disregarded in the interests of an almost exclusive concentration on what is variously called integrity, "engagement," or self-development. This is not to say that these are not, all of them, highly desirable values, or virtues, as the case may be, but they do not constitute the whole of the subject matter of ethics. Virtues— such as justice—the community, law and the like must still be considered. The view of Aristotle and St. Thomas (and for that matter of Plato and Hegel) that ethics is concerned with acts in a social setting cannot be disregarded. For example, when we hear such expressions as "he is very involved," or "he is very dedicated," or "he is very concerned," or "he is very sincere," we should notice, in the first place, that none of these words is substantive—they all qualify nouns, and without nouns they tell us very little. "Involved": in what? blackmail? collecting stamps? breeding canaries? "Dedicated": to what? making money? to the pursuit of pleasure? to reading "Li'l Abner"? "Concerned": with what or whom? with the poor? with the rich? with his little old grandmother in the country? Finally, "sincere": he is a sincere what? politician, Führer? janitor? or what? In other words, even a superficial analysis of language ought

to show us that there is something seriously wrong
with a view of moral philosophy which is content
with throwing the incense of words expressing general
approval instead of analysing man in his actual social
relationships.

Similarly the faith of a Christian is not merely his
own integrity, nor is it his bravery in the face of the
mystery of existence, nor is it his effort to become
truly an individual; it is also a faith he believes with
other people, and which bears on the way he must
treat other people. This common faith is possible only
because there is an institution which proclaims the
faith we share with others, and which unites us to
others whether they be "like-minded" or not. It is
within this institution, this structured community, that
the effort is made to live the Christian faith. You cannot have Catholicism without the institution any more
than you can have an adequate ethical theory without
considering the individual in his social relationships,
and the world in which he acts.

The point, of course, that Catholicism has always
understood itself as a visible structured community
is not seriously contested by anyone. It is the claim
of the Church, it is the reproach levelled at her by
those who disagree with her. It is argued that this view
which the Church has of herself is a distortion of the
religion of Christ as found in the New Testament.
Here is where the controversy is to be found. The
Germans even invented a word, *Frühkatholizismus*—
early Catholicism—as a term of reproach for those
who saw any trace of the Catholic idea of the Church
in the New Testament. The discussion as to whether
or not the Church in the Epistles is institutional or not
is a question for the experts and will be dealt with in
a subsequent paper; here I will content myself with a

quotation from the Anglican scholar, Dr. Stephen Neill:

If there is one thing more certain than another about these early churches, it is that admission to them was by faith and *baptism*. The New Testament knows nothing of membership in the Church by faith alone, without the accompanying act of obedience and confession. The Epistle to the Romans was probably written in A.D. 56, that is, less than thirty years after the death of Christ; Paul takes it for granted that all his readers will have been baptized, and that the extraordinary high and realistic doctrine of baptism which he presents to them is the familiar tradition of the Church and not a strange new doctrine which he has himself thought up under the influence of some Hellenistic tradition or other. Whether we like it or not, from the very beginning the Christian Church, which had grown out of the Jewish Church, had its institutional element. We may say, if we wish, that baptism was merely the outward expression of a living faith, and that faith was the all-important thing. This is true, but it does not alter the fact that, until faith had found its expression in baptism, the believer was not a member of the Christian community, the body of Christ. Non-sacramental Christianity, as it is found today in almost all the Protestant churches of the Continent of Europe, is an invention of the rationalistic nineteenth century; it has little to do with the Christianity of the New Testament and cannot be made to square with it.[7]

Suppose, however, that we concede the historical point that Catholic Christianity has always considered itself as social and institutional; is it not possible this has been a terrible mistake? What, after all, has the real, true meaning of the Gospel got to do with the antique institution weighed down by the centuries which we call the Church, an institution bearing the marks of ancient controversies and the scars of often questionable when not sinful behaviour; what has this institution, stumbling from age to age, reeling under the impact of the most diverse ideologies and cultures, what has this antique institution we call the Church of Rome got to do with the coming, great, purified Church of the future?

Stripped of its rhetoric this question forces us to ask ourselves whether or not we believe God has acted in history through a Church. If we do believe that the Church is the way Christ's mercy goes on being made real through the structured community which administers the sacraments and teaches the faith, then we have to accept the consequence that, whatever ecclesiastical reformations there may be, there must be a recognizable identity between these results and the Church of the Apostles and martyrs, of the Fathers and the Doctors, of the Counter-reformation and of more recent times. Christianity as understood by the Church is tied down to history and is best understood in the light of the revealing, the self-giving of God in Christ. It is to this community, lawfully constituted as a society, that the fulness of revelation in Christ remains present in the world as reality and truth. The power and spirit of Christ working through time is directed towards the building up of a community of believers, the mystical body of Jesus Christ. The *Dogmatic Constitution on the Church* of the Second Vatican Council expressed this belief in the following way:

> Christ, the one Mediator, established and ceaselessly sustains here on earth His holy Church, the community of faith, hope and charity, as a visible structure. Through her He communicates truth and grace to all. But the society furnished with hierarchical agencies and the Mystical Body of Christ are not to be considered as two reali-

ties, nor are the visible assembly and the spiritual community, nor the earthly Church and the Church enriched by heavenly things. Rather they form one interlocked reality which is comprised of a divine and a human element. For this reason, by an excellent analogy, this reality is compared to the mystery of the incarnate Word. Just as the assumed nature inseparably united to the divine Word serves Him as a living instrument of salvation, so, in a similar way, does the communal structure of the Church serve Christ's Spirit, who vivifies it by way of building up the body.[8]

We Catholics, then, are committed to the view that the Church is not some sort of invisible reality, without any palpable structure, but that it is a communion which is a visible, historical, and organized society endowed with the power of government. It is the judgment of Fr. de Lubac that the ecclesiology of contemporary Catholicism is on this fundamental point in perfect continuity with the ecclesiology of the first Christian centuries.[9] This appeal to authority may not be the strongest of arguments, but it seems worthwhile to repeat the point that the world of the great theologians and of the council is very far removed from what we are often told.

In thinking about our faith and our Church we must always return to the principle that we are dealing with a mystery, the mystery of God's dealing with men. We are not dealing with a philosophy, or a scheme of ideas which we might have thought up. We believe that God became a man to share His life with us, and we must try to see the mystery of the Church in the light of this faith.

The Church, then, is important, not because it has certain quasi-legal sorts of claims on our obedience, but because it is the community willed by Christ, the

members of which share in an explicit way fellowship
with one another as partakers of our Lord's risen life.
And this, I suppose, is important because we believe
that the mystery of human life and death can only be
understood in the mystery of the life and death and
resurrection of Jesus Christ.

DOGMATIC

One of the elements which make possible the common
faith and unity of the Church is the dogmatic element
in Christianity. The words dogma and dogmatic have
not got very happy overtones in modern English.
They are words usually associated with an overween-
ing, arrogant cast of mind or mode of speech. The
word itself in Greek, however, means "what seems
right," and in the New Testament it usually means a
decree or a decision. For example, in the Acts of the
Apostles we read "They delivered to them for observance the decisions which had been reached by the
Apostles"—the decisions, τα δόγματα.[10] The character
of dogma can only be understood within this social
and ecclesial setting, because the revelation under-
lying dogma was made to the Church, a group of people, and not to a number of unrelated individuals.

If we are to appreciate adequately the importance
of the dogmatic element in Christianity we must remember that Catholicism claims to find its source in a
revelation. The writer of the Epistle to the Hebrews
says "that in many and various ways God spoke of old
to our fathers, by the prophets, but in these last days
He has spoken to us by the Son." [11] In this passage
we have the kernel of the idea of revelation—it is a
movement from God to man. "In His goodness and
wisdom," the council says, "God chose to reveal Himself and make known the hidden purpose of His

will . . . ; through this revelation, therefore, the invisible God out of the abundance of His love speaks to men as friends." [12]

The response to revelation on the part of mankind is faith:

"The obedience of faith" must be given to God who reveals, an obedience by which man entrusts his whole self to God, offering "the full submission of intellect and will to God who reveals," and freely assenting to the truth revealed by Him.[13]

The revelation which is accepted by faith is, we believe, committed to the Church. The revelation was not meant for the exclusive edification of the first generation of Christians but was given to be handed on. It was given to the Apostles and was to be delivered to all generations by their successors who were to draw on what had been given to the Apostles. What was given to the Apostles is found in one sacred deposit of the word of God which comprises Scripture and tradition, and "the task of authentically interpreting the word of God, whether written or handed on, has been entrusted exclusively to the living teaching office of the Church, whose authority is exercised in the name of Jesus Christ." [14]

The Dutch Catechism sums up these points in the following incisive way:

Faith comes by hearing. It is not something one discovers for oneself. It cannot be attained by analysing the nature of man. No. One accepts something that one has not seen. One hears what Christ imparts from the Father. One hears it through the word of the Church.[15]

Nothing in what I have just said is meant to be anything more than a reminder of what we all believe. We believe that Christianity is a revelation, that this revelation was committed to the Church, and that parts of this revelation have been expressed in words or propositions called dogma. It is, however, important to realize that this position involves two principles or consequences which are widely rejected today: that dogma is unalterable, and that it is accepted on authority. What the Church taught in the fourth century is still true, and we know it was and is true, because it is taught by the Church. This does not mean that there is no room for the development in our understanding of what has been affirmed, but it does mean, very definitely, that what has been affirmed as a statement or proposition expressing the judgment of the Church about what has been revealed must be accepted as the Church understood the proposition.

We ought to be clear, I think, that not only unbelievers, but a great many Christians of the liberal tradition would reject this claim. Hegel as a young man, for example, wrote in an essay called the "Positivity of the Christian Religion" that "great men have claimed that the fundamental meaning of Protestant is a man or a Church which has not bound itself to certain unalterable standards of faith, but which protests against all authority in matters of belief." [16] This quotation from the *fons et origo* of so much of modern Protestant thought is of interest to us because it expresses a certain cast of mind which is all around us today. This cast of mind identifies religion which is sincere—and therefore, I suppose, true—with a kind of striving towards the truth, and the absence of anything fixed or definite. The value of this striving seems usually to be judged in moral terms, and moral terms not in the sense of a concern for the common good, but as personal integrity and self-development. It is clear that if we look on religion this way the accept-

ance of truth on authority will be rejected—it might
interfere with self-development. And so Hegel with
his usual genius for description has very accurately
outlined a position which is so widespread that it
needs to be articulated before most of us are even
aware that we are faced with a point of view which
is diametrically opposed to Catholic Christianity. It
may go against the grain to say that we receive our
faith as something to be accepted on authority, as
something given; nonetheless, when we read or hear
that there are no unalterable standards of faith, or
that faith has nothing to do with the Church, let us
realize that the view is un-Catholic and not particularly new.

Today, under the influence of existentialist currents
of thought, we have come to appreciate better that
revelation as delivered to the Church is much more
than a series of propositions to which we give an intellectual assent. Such words as "encounter" and "saving event" are on the lips of a great many people. My
acceptance of the truth of Christ, it is said, is uniquely
different from that of anyone else because God loves
each one of us, and constitutes each one of us, and
therefore speaks to each one of us, in quite a different
way. We cannot, however, accept this as the whole
story. No doubt revelation is a great deal more than
a bundle of propositions or sentences which state a
number of truths in a way which our intellect can
understand; but this should not be taken to mean that
suddenly revelation does not say anything at all. The
idea that God reveals, but does not reveal anything in
particular, is a very odd one; that He reveals what
once was true but no longer is, seems even odder. No,
Christianity is social in its character. Revelation was
committed to the Church, and the dogmas which ex-

press this revelation, and the sentences and propositions which in part contain it, are what make possible
the common belief of the Church.

Newman wrote:

> It seems to have been the duty of every individual Chris-
> tian from the first to witness in his place against all opin-
> ions which were contrary to what he had received in his
> baptismal catechizing, and to shun the society of those
> who maintained them. . . . Such a principle, however,
> would but have broken up the Church the sooner, resolv-
> ing it into the individuals of which it was composed,
> unless the truth, to which they were to bear witness, had
> been a something definite, and formal, and independent
> of themselves. Christians were bound to defend and trans-
> mit the faith which they had received, and they received
> it from the rulers of the Church; and on the other hand,
> it was the duty of those rulers to watch over and define
> this traditionary faith.[17]

The function of the Church, then, in its teaching authority is to guard, transmit, and explain the divine
revelation which came in Jesus Christ at a given point
in history. Its function, however, is not to be understood as a sort of gramophone which goes on repeating
the original revelation as though it were merely something given long ago. The Church has to present
revelation as something which takes place "now," as
something proclaimed by the living voice of the
Church to be appropriated by the contemporary believer.[18] It stands to reason that if Christianity is a
universal religion which was not designed merely to
satisfy the needs of one particular age, place, or ethnic
group, but was meant for all times, places, and peoples,
then it must vary in its relation and dealings towards
the world around it, and this is another way of saying
that it must develop. Principles require different sorts

of application as persons and circumstances vary, and
therefore must be put into new forms according to
the type of society which they are to influence.[19]

The whole question of development as distinct from
mere change is a complex and difficult one, and is not
our central concern here. This reference to development, however, ought to remind us that we cannot
expect the Church to remain static, that continuity is
no more a mark of the Church than the adaption and
development required to make Christ's saving truth
meaningful for every age. Modes of expression do
grow old, and often they seem to have little relevance
to preaching the word of God in contemporary circumstances. Karl Rahner has reminded us that to do
nothing in such a case is an indication of indifference
to that very truth one wishes to defend. It betrays a
lack of power of appropriation and of practical as-
similation which he does not hesitate to call heresy,
"a heresy in which dead orthodoxy is merely the result and the expression of an inner indifference towards truth." [20] A lifeless mechanical voicing of propositions is no substitute for a living faith, but this is
not to say that for a living faith propositions are not
a vital necessity.

In sum, then, we believe Christianity is a relevation
which is committed to the Church. Part of this revelation is expressed in the form of propositions or dogmas
which in turn make possible the social character of
Christianity. These dogmas develop so they may be
made relevant to the different ages and cultures within
which the Church lives.

Some may be tempted to wonder what this dry and, I
am afraid, at times even technical discussion of the
Church as social and dogmatic has to do with the

needs of our own day. When we consider the extent
of unbelief around us, the apparent confusion which
exists in the Church itself, the dreariness of so much
of human existence, surely a discussion such as we
have been having is little more than a retreat into
scholasticism—rather like playing Chinese chequers or
doing formal logic—a flight from the real problems
facing mankind into a world of theory which has little
to do with the realities of life.

We have said the faith, being intended for all ages,
is social and dogmatic, that revelation was committed
to the Church, and that what was so committed has
been expressed over the ages in the form of statements
or decisions which we call dogma. The moment we
have said this, however, there is a sense that the essential has been missed. It will be said even if the faith is
social and dogmatic and intended for all ages that we
will not convert the world with this sort of language.

First of all, it must be pointed out in reply, that converting the world is a somewhat extensive operation,
involving, one would imagine, a number of different
aspects, and different types of endeavour; among
which, presumably, an attempt to understand will find
its place. I have not been trying here to explain the
whole of what the Church understands by Christianity, nor to solve the problems of atheism and the salvation of the unbeliever, nor, most assuredly, to speak
on catechetics. All I have been trying to do is to set
the stage for the coming papers by recalling to your
minds certain fundamentals of our Catholic view of
Christianity. But this particular criticism is only an
instance of an attitude which cannot be reprobated too
strongly—the tendency to condemn any attempt at
quiet, rational discussion as scholastic or formalistic.

We should notice that in themselves the words

"scholastic" and "formalistic" are not necessarily terms
of abuse. To treat them as such is often an indication
of the presence of a contempt or disregard for reason,
and we find a great deal of this in contemporary writing. There are those who, in a no doubt very laudable
desire to preach the Gospel and make the Church
more open to the world, show a marked aversion to
careful argument, or indeed to any argument what-
soever.

This sort of anti-intellectualism must be rejected out
of hand; in the first place, because reason is considered
by the Church to be important in the way we accept
the faith. Even if we are unwilling to define man by
his capacity to use his mind, it would, nonetheless,
take a very brave existentialist to hold that man was
mindless. It is part of the Catholic view of faith that
reason has a role to play in our believing. So I think
that within the tradition of the Church the attitude of
suspicion towards what is termed "scholastic" is un-
sound.

This sort of argument cannot, however, be expected
to cut very much ice today. I would add, then, that
practically speaking the attempt to bypass reason can
only end in disaster. The scholastic attitude towards
reality in the late Middle Ages was shown by A. N.
Whitehead to have been the attitude which made possible the rise of modern science. That is, the careful
attempt to analyse, define, and recognize things as they
are, and the respect for objectivity or reality which
this entails, is the same intellectual prerequisite demanded by the scientific method. And more generally,
the attempt to shortcut reason ends up in a blind alley,
because even the most profound insights, even the
most sincere "engagement avec les problèmes actuels
du monde," even the most audacious appreciation and

going-out to the values of the secular world, will get us nowhere unless there is some attempt to collate, define, and understand what is being done, and to judge whether or not what is so defined and understood is in fact going to be of assistance in preaching the faith. It is often true that those who are most vocal in preaching openness to the world are the harshest critics of that very reason which has made possible the existence of the modern world. No doubt reason has been abused at times, overemphasized, employed in areas and in ways which showed little sensitivity to the complexities of the subject matter; no doubt all this and a great deal more is true, but this does not alter the fact that it is still necessary for theology and religion. To refuse reason its rights is to earn the contempt of the world we are trying to influence, and to run the risk of turning the Christian message into a series of contradictory trivialities which in fact are little more than an expression of that utilitarianism and vague good will which is the unofficial, but very real, philosophy of this continent.

Here I would like to add a plea for a respect for words and definitions. What would we think of a physicist who changed his definitions half way through an experiment, but assured us he found self-fulfillment in his work? Or a doctor who took out a pancreas instead of an appendix because he was not careful enough to read the medical report, but insisted that he was very involved? Or a chartered accountant who gave us the gross receipts when we wanted the profits, and who told us what mattered was interest in his work, and that we should not get "hung up" on definitions? We would probably say our physicist was incompetent, our doctor criminally irresponsible, and our accountant just plain criminal. But when it comes

to theology, or ecumenical endeavours, it seems that
a cavalier treatment of words is to be found all around
us, and it can lead to nothing but confusion, frustration, and bad temper, and to the weakening—not the
strengthening—of the Christian witness before the
world. This is altogether apart from the fact that we
are supposed to be dealing with realities as important
as the experiments of the physicist, the pancreas, and
the balance sheet.

It is not obscurantism or being old-fashioned to
maintain that an attempt at clarity in theological language is indispensable. It does not show a lack of
sincerity to hold that language is a necessary vehicle
through which we understand and say what can be
said about God, Christ, the Church, sin and redemption. One does not suddenly become an essentialist—
whatever that means—because one holds that faith is
not simply ineffable response, but is social and must
therefore be expressed in propositions which do not
falsify it, even if they do not exhaust its meaning.

Finally, we return to the point from which we
started, which was the need for a deeper loyalty to
the Church if we are to live our lives in faith. The
Church is where we find Christ, it is Christianity as
it is lived in reality, not as an idea. Our efforts to
understand better the Church and her nature will result in a deeper understanding and a higher valuation
of our faith. For the faith about which we have spoken
is not faith in the abstract, but faith in Christ, in the
living God who is presented to us through the Church,
in her teaching and in her sacraments—the same
Church which at the council tried to give us a new
standpoint from which to present the Gospel in a way
relevant to our own times, the Church which sought
to show that the mystical body was the home for all

mankind, including the often perplexed, anguished, and alienated modern, educated Catholic. Yet it remains a fact, somehow or other, that this post-conciliar period has witnessed an orgy of self-criticism by Catholics. Everything Catholic is by definition suspect, the old ways are corrupt, the new ones of last week are out of date.

Even when we admit, as we must, that sinful human nature, shortsightedness, a failure to act for the needs of the present, as well as to plan for the future, have all characterized the office bearers of the Church, still, there seems to be a bitterness abroad which often appears incommensurate with its cause. That leaders all too often do not lead is, alas, all too true, but each one of us has to ask himself the question about who has the right to throw the first stone. Even if everything said about authority in the Church is true, there is still the further matter of our own particular contribution. "Do we not, each one of us, belong to the tired grey company who obscure the light of the Gospel by their mediocrity, their cowardice, and their egoism?" [21] We must not avoid answering this question by writing week after week, year in and year out, about the ineptitude of our leaders. St. Catherine of Siena and St. Theresa of Avila did not mince their words when it came to dealing with authority, even the papacy, and yet the ground of it all was a flaming love for Christ and His Church which reconciled people to the very institution they criticized. This aspect of the matter is not especially evident today.

If the Church is failing to convert the world, is it not perhaps because we have failed to convert ourselves? Unless we try to grow in the knowledge and love of Christ which we can never do without prayer and sacrament then the Church will never appear before the world as she really is, and the fault will, in no small measure, be our own.

In conclusion I would like to quote the closing lines of Cardinal Léger's last major discourse in Canada which he delivered to the Theology Congress at Toronto in August, 1967:

We must never forget that the Spirit which gives us life is the Spirit of holiness and that the great lack of the contemporary world is that hunger of the soul for God without which there will be a return to a barbarism which could so quickly replace the highest forms of civilized life. History contains many lessons which could help us to grasp the true meaning of renewal in the Church. Let us hope that the historians of the future who will examine our times will discover in them that wisdom which flowered into true contemplation. It is contemplation which enriches the robes of the Church, the pure spouse of Christ, which He bought with His blood. It is contemplation which kills our selfishness and allows us to express that unity which Christ made clear was the distinctive mark of His Church: that they may be one, Father, even as you and I are one. It is by contemplation that we find our way into the room of the bride, where Christ speaks to each one of us in an individual, incommunicable way; and in which He says all with the words "I have loved you with an everlasting love." [22]

NOTES

1. Romans 1:17.
2. Ronald Knox, "Absolute and Abitofhell," in *Essays in Satire* (New York: Dutton, 1930).
3. John Henry Cardinal Newman, *An Essay on the Development of Christian Doctrine* (London: Longmans, 1897), Ch. II, sec. 2, no. 13.
4. Henri de Lubac, s.j., "*Lumen Gentium* and the Fathers," in *Vatican II: An Interfaith Appraisal* (Notre Dame: University of Notre Dame Press, 1966).

5. E.g., John 8:31, 17:17.
6. Edward Schillebeeckx, o.p., *Vatican II: The Real Achievement*, translated by H. J. J. Vaughan (New York: Herder and Herder, 1967), Ch. 3, sec. 3.
7. Stephen Neill, *The Interpretation of the New Testament, 1861–1961* (London: Collins, 1966), Ch. 5, sec. 2.
8. *Documents of Vatican II*, general editor Walter M. Abbott, s.j. (New York: Herder & Herder, and Association Press, 1966), p. 22.
9. de Lubac, *op. cit.*, sec. 2.
10. Acts 16:4.
11. Hebrews 1:1.
12. *Documents of Vatican II*, p. 112.
13. *Ibid.*, p. 113.
14. *Ibid.*, pp. 117–118.
15. "Faith Comes by Hearing," in *A New Catechism* (New York: Herder and Herder, 1966).
16. G. W. F. Hegel, "Positivity of the Christian Religion," in *Early Theological Writings*, translated by T. M. Knox (Chicago: University of Chicago Press, 1948), p. 128.
17. Newman, *op. cit.*, Ch. VII, sec. 5, nos. 2 and 3.
18. Karl Rahner, s.j., "Considerations on the Development of Dogma," in *Theological Investigations* (Baltimore: Helicon, 1961), Vol. IV.
19. Newman, *op. cit.*, Ch. II, sec. 1, no. 3.
20. Karl Rahner, s.j., "What is Heresy?" in *op. cit.*, Vol. V.
21. Karl Rahner, s.j., "Thoughts on the Possibility of Belief Today," in *op cit.*, Vol. V.
22. Paul-Émile Cardinal Léger, "The Theology of the Renewal of the Church," in *The Theology of Renewal* (Montreal: Palm, 1968), Vol. I.

2

The Interpretation of the
New Testament Today

William Henry Irwin, c.s.b.

WHAT HAS THE INTERPRETATION of the New Testament to do with the faith in today's world? The answer is simple. It is precisely in the New Testament that the faith we are talking about is first found written down and guaranteed by God's authority.

[The Church] has always regarded the Scriptures together with sacred tradition as the supreme rule of faith, and will ever do so. For, inspired by God and committed once and for all to writing, they impart the word of God Himself without change, and make the voice of the Holy Spirit resound in the words of the prophets and apostles.

These are the words of the Second Vatican Council.[1] If we take them seriously, then the interpretation of the New Testament becomes a very important matter for the faith at any time and certainly for the faith in today's world. Any significant change in the interpretation of the New Testament must affect the faith. Nor can we dispense with interpretation. The language the New Testament was written in is not our own. It must be translated for us. Translation must then be supplemented by commentary since the men of two thousand years ago had ways of expressing themselves which sometimes seem strange and obscure to us, even when what they have written has been translated. Yet translation supplemented by commentary is not enough. The New Testament is not, for the Christian, something simply to be understood; it is something to be believed, to be guided by, to die for. Therefore, we must go beyond the question of the sense of the New Testament to the question of the truth of the New Testament.

Is there a difference between sense and truth? For the fundamentalist there is not. For him to know what the Bible says is to know what he must believe. It was this attitude which left the Church wide-open to the attacks of critics of the Bible who exposed, for example, the naïveté with which it viewed the age of the world and of man or the exaggeration with which it counted the numbers who had departed Egypt in the Exodus. These critical attacks forced the Church to re-examine her position vis-à-vis the scriptures and to recall what she had really known all along, that the Bible is a religious book and the truth that matters in it is the religious truth.

The Second Vatican Council puts it this way. The truth which the books of Scripture must be acknowledged as teaching firmly, faithfully, and without error is "that truth which God wanted put into the sacred writings for the sake of our salvation." [2] The scriptures are not a textbook in natural science, or geography, or the history of Palestine and related areas. They teach with divine authority what God chose to reveal and record for the salvation of mankind. It is this truth of salvation which finally is the object of New Testament interpretation. And it is to problems relating to this truth of the New Testament that I wish to address myself.

I will begin with a look at a recent theory of New Testament interpretation that goes by the name of "demythologizing." It was proposed in 1941 by a German Protestant, Rudolf Bultmann, but it was brought to the attention of the English-speaking public by the little book of John Robinson entitled *Honest to God*. As far as I can determine, *Honest to God* caused many Catholic priests and laymen to "discover" Bultmann. His ideas are worth knowing because of their current popularity and because in his own way he tackles the question of the truth of the New Testament today. His theory depends very much, in fact, on his conception of the central message of the New Testament.

In the second part of this paper I will turn to a more traditional conception of the truth of the New Testament as it is embodied in the creeds of the Church. My purpose will not be to examine the creeds in detail, but rather to compare their understanding of the truth of salvation with that found in the gospel. The third section will then deal with the role of the Church in the transmission, interpretation, and preservation of the truth of salvation. I do not intend myself to present a new interpretation of the gospel message. I hope rather to highlight certain fundamental principles useful in testing the soundness of any new interpretation.

I

DEMYTHOLOGIZING THE NEW TESTAMENT

I referred above to the "discovery" of Bultmann by
Catholics. This would hardly have been possible without the encouragement given by the Second Vatican
Council to the study of "literary genres" as an aid to
interpretation of the Bible. After reaffirming the divine
authority of the scriptures the *Dogmatic Constitution
on Divine Revelation* continues:

However, since God speaks in sacred Scripture through
men in human fashion, the interpreter of sacred Scripture, in order to see clearly what God wanted to communicate to us, should carefully investigate what meaning the sacred writers really intended, and what God
wanted to manifest by means of their words.

Those who search out the intention of the sacred
writers must, among other things, have regard for "literary forms." For truth is proposed and expressed in a
variety of ways, depending on whether a text is history
of one kind or another, or whether its form is that of
prophecy, poetry, or some other type of speech. The
interpreter must investigate what meaning the sacred
writer intended to express and actually expressed in particular circumstances as he used contemporary literary
forms in accordance with the situation of his own time
and culture.[3]

This is an important text. It takes with utmost seriousness the proposition that God speaks to us in the
scriptures *through men*. We are instructed that it is
by investigating the meaning which the sacred writer
intended to express and actually expressed in particular circumstances that we may see clearly what God
wanted to communicate to us. Furthermore, we are

told to pay special attention to "literary forms," "for truth is proposed and expressed in a variety of ways, depending on whether a text is history of one kind or another or whether its form is that of prophecy, poetry, or some other type of speech." This is an important text, as I have said, because it enables the interpreter of the Bible to take full account of the human element therein without thereby detracting from its divine authority.

Now, how does this concern the theory of Bultmann? In this way: fundamental to his thesis is the assertion that "myth" is the literary form in which the central message of the New Testament is cast. His entire reinterpretation of the New Testament depends on this assertion, and this he must prove. For it is one thing to admit that one must interpret the New Testament giving due attention to the literary forms used by its authors; it is quite another thing to assert that the New Testament authors actually used the literary form "myth."

Let us follow his argument.[4] Bultmann draws our attention to the problem of preaching the gospel to modern man. When modern man reads the New Testament he finds himself confronted by a world of angels and demons, of miracle and magic, of a dying and rising God, and modern man recognizes this conception of the world to be a mythological one, one which has passed from the scene with the rise of modern science. This, then, is the situation: modern man is prevented from listening to the gospel and from giving it his faith because of its old-fashioned world view.

The Christian preacher is faced, then, by the question: to call this man to faith must I call him to believe in this outdated world, this mythological world, or is the essential message of the New Testament distinguishable from its mythology?

His answer is *yes*. The essential message of Christianity does not irretrievably depend upon the acceptance of the mythological world view in which it is represented. First, the positive value of myth must be appreciated—myth is not simply something false; it is not just an old cosmology to be replaced by modern science. The real purpose of myth is not to give an explanation of the world as it is but rather to express an understanding of human existence.

Myth is an expression of man's conviction that the origin and purpose of the world in which he lives are to be sought not within it but beyond it—that is, beyond the realm of known and tangible reality—and that this realm is perpetually dominated and menaced by those mysterious powers which are its source and limit. Myth is also an expression of man's awareness that he is not lord of his own being. It expresses his sense of dependence not only within the visible world, but more especially on those forces which hold sway beyond the confines of the known. Finally, myth expresses man's belief that in this state of dependence he can be delivered from the forces within the visible world.[5]

Myth expresses this understanding, however, not by abstract language but by representing the otherworldly, that which is in Bultmann's words "beyond the confines of the known" as a this-worldly reality. As examples we could cite miracle stories, stories of possession by demons, stories of gods walking the earth in human form. In all these examples what is typical is that the other-worldly powers become visible; they enter into this world and seem to take their place alongside all the other realities of this world. Now, once these stories are recognized as myth one realizes that the depiction of these other-worldly realities as objective realities in this world is not to be taken literally. In fact, to take myth literally in this way is to draw attention away from its real meaning for human existence.

It is Bultmann's contention that the New Testament expresses its message of salvation in mythical language understood in this sense. Thus to interpret the message of the New Testament properly one must recognize this fact and seek the true sense of that message in the understanding of existence which it expresses. When the New Testament depicts Satan, sin, and death as powers which rule over this world, he tells us, it wishes to convey by myth that man apart from faith is captive to his own selfishness to which he becomes a slave by seeking his true existence in the tangible rewards of this world. When man chooses to live entirely in and for this sphere of visible, concrete, tangible, and measurable reality, which as such is also the sphere of corruption and death, this sphere assumes the shape of a "power." To this mode of existence the New Testament opposes the alternative, again in mythical language, of the life of faith. This life is based on unseen, intangible, realities—specifically, it is based upon God's love which confronts a man and offers him the possibility of living a new life freed from bondage to this world of tangible realities and transitory objects which shuts out invisible reality from our lives.[6]

What characterizes the New Testament message as original is its answer to the question whether this new life for man can be realized or not. Philosophy assumes that man by his own efforts can enter upon this new mode of existing. The New Testament states categorically that this is impossible. This is the meaning of the doctrine of sin. The fall is total, and hence man cannot achieve his true being. It is precisely his conviction that he can achieve himself by his own efforts which is the sin that cuts him off from the new life.

The message which the New Testament proclaims is that God has acted when man was powerless to help himself. God now offers man the possibility of that new existence if he will only abandon all self-sought security in total confidence in the love of God which embraces and sustains him even in his fallen, self-assertive state. Note that the New Testament does not simply proclaim that it is necessary for God to offer man this possibility of new life because man cannot achieve it by his own efforts. It proclaims that God, in fact, has offered this possibility. That is why what is preached is Christ, the saving event. In the preaching of the Christ-event the love of God actually confronts men and calls them to make a decision to accept or reject the message: to abandon all security in this world for God, or to refuse God by relying on human security.

I have dwelt at some length on this interpretation by Bultmann of the essential message of the New Testament; there is a good reason for this. His method of demythologizing the New Testament starts with this definition of the essential message of the New Testament—that is to say, he starts with his creed and proceeds to show how the New Testament should be interpreted so that this creed may be seen to be its central message.

Let us watch him at work in interpreting the resurrection of Jesus. The resurrection to Bultmann is obviously a myth: modern man finds it incredible that a man should come back to life; in addition, we find many stories of dying and rising gods in antiquity, and

INTERPRETATION OF THE NEW TESTAMENT TODAY 47

we do not hesitate to call them myths. In the New Testament, however, we have a unique combination of myth and history. The life of Jesus of Nazareth is more than just a myth. It is a human life which ended in crucifixion. But alongside the historical event of the crucifixion the New Testament sets the definitely non-historical event of the resurrection. Since this is the case

we are compelled to ask whether all this mythological language is not simply an attempt to express the meaning of the historical figure of Jesus and the events of his life; in other words, the significance of these as a figure and event of salvation. If that be so, we can dispense with the objective form in which they are cast.[7]

In fact, if we look at the New Testament we see that it is interested in the resurrection of Christ simply and solely because the resurrection is the event *par excellence* which saves us, what Bultmann calls the eschatological event. Now as eschatological event it is revelation of the essential message of the New Testament, i.e., God offers us the possibility of dying to our old life and rising to a new life. It is this meaning of the resurrection for our lives that the New Testament is interested in.

Bultmann admits that the New Testament treats the resurrection also as a miraculous proof of the message. Paul himself attempts such a proof in 1 Corinthians 15. But, Bultmann remarks, this is a dangerous procedure. Not only because an historical fact which involves a resurrection from the dead is utterly inconceivable, but also because the resurrection itself is an object of faith, and one cannot prove one object of faith from another.

If the event of Easter Day is in any sense an historical

event additional to the event of the cross, it is nothing else than the rise of faith in the risen Lord, since it was this faith which led to the apostolic preaching.[8]

One might object: "are you not by your demythologizing destroying all objective bases for Christian faith?" Bultmann will certainly reply, "Yes, indeed." Faith can have no other basis than itself. The ground and object of faith are identical. I believe the word of God because it is the word of God, and I recognize it as the word of God by faith. You can see that in Bultmann both skepticism and fideism come in strong doses. In fact, for him his skepticism is a predisposition for faith.

Our radical attempt to de-mythologize the N[ew] T[estament] is in fact a perfect parallel to St. Paul's and Luther's doctrine of justification by faith alone apart from the works of the Law. Or rather, it carries this doctrine to its logical conclusion in the field of epistemology. Like the doctrine of justification it destroys every false security and every false demand for it on the part of man, whether he seeks it in his good works or in his ascertainable knowledge. The man who wishes to believe in God as his God must realize that he has nothing in his hand on which to base his faith. He is suspended in mid-air, and cannot demand a proof of the Word which addresses him. For the ground and object of faith are identical. Security can be found only by abandoning all security, by being ready, as Luther put it, to plunge into the inner darkness.[9]

There you have in brief outline demythologizing and its justification. We have seen what happens to the traditional doctrine of the resurrection of Jesus in this new interpretation, and this should at least give us pause and cause us to consider with more attention the assertion basic to the method, that myth is used by the

New Testament to express its message. I think that if you accept this then you must go quite a way with Bultmann. Let me put it plainly: if the resurrection in the central message of the New Testament is a myth, then one is perfectly justified in abandoning a literal belief in the account of Jesus' resurrection from the dead.

Critique. Has Bultmann proved his case? Does the New Testament use myth the way he says it does? That is the crucial question because, as I have just said, give Bultmann this and you cannot deny him the conclusions he draws. Some have criticized him for saying that we can dispense with myth once we have discovered its meaning. The authors who take this line insist that myth must always play a role in Christian proclamation of the message of salvation because of the peculiar religious character of that message. No doubt this criticism scores a point against Bultmann, but it leaves untouched the fundamental issue because it accepts the assertion that one may properly speak of the New Testament message as myth.

Now unless one takes "myth" in an altogether trivial sense as the use of imaginative, metaphorical language (which no one would deny the Bible is full of), it makes a very big difference in your understanding of the New Testament whether you hold that myth is its primary mode of expression, or not. The reason is this: whether you take Bultmann's definition of myth or some much more sophisticated one, in order for de-mythologizing to work at all it must be agreed that the real purpose of the myth is the expression of man's understanding of the intangible, invisible, other-worldly realities of his world and that its expression of this understanding is the *truth* of the myth. All else is mode of expression. Again let me put it bluntly: when the New Testament says that Jesus rose from the dead, it does not mean that Jesus of Nazareth who had been crucified on the cross came back to life. That is not the truth it wishes to express; rather, the truth it proclaims is that God is now offering us new life. Because of the time and culture of the New Testament authors they chose to tell us this by means of the myth of Jesus' resurrection from the dead.

We will want very good arguments, indeed, from Professor Bultmann, then, if he expects us to agree that the message of the New Testament is made in myth. What are his arguments? They can be divided into two classes: arguments against the literal truth of the resurrection, and arguments in favor of the myth-ological interpretation. In the first class are all those arguments which prove that the resurrection could not happen. Characteristically Bultmann finds that such a miracle is contrary not only to reason but to faith:

The resurrection of Jesus cannot be a miraculous proof by which the sceptic might be compelled to believe in Christ. The difficulty is not simply the incredibility of a mythical event like the resuscitation of a dead person— for that is what the resurrection means as is shown by the fact that the risen Lord is apprehended by the physical senses. Nor is it merely the impossibility of establishing the objective historicity of the resurrection no matter how many witnesses are cited, as though once it was established it might be believed beyond all question and faith might have its unimpreachable guarantee. No; the real difficulty is that the resurrection is itself an article of faith, and you cannot establish one article of faith by invoking another. You cannot prove the redemptive ef-ficacy of the cross by invoking the resurrection. For the resurrection is an article of faith because it is far more than the resuscitation of a corpse—it is the eschatological event. And so it cannot be a miraculous proof. For, quite apart from its credibility, the bare miracle tells us nothing about the eschatological fact of the destruction of death.[10]

Now this argument, insofar as it contains anything more than the fashionable prejudice against miracle, depends upon an understanding of miracle according to which miracle is by definition a contradiction of faith. It is what compels a skeptic to believe in Christ. Such an obviously loaded conception of miracle casts doubt not only on the truth of his argument, but on its seriousness as well.

For the New Testament this supposed contradiction between miracle and faith does not exist at all. According to the New Testament the resurrection is both miracle and eschatological event. It is not proof which compels the skeptic to believe. Thomas the Doubter saw the Lord and he believed, but what he saw bore no comparison at all with what he believed when he confessed, "My Lord, and my God."

The real point at issue is this: do the New Testament witnesses testify to having seen the risen Jesus in bodily form; do they testify that the resurrection of this Jesus they had seen is the eschatological event? If they do so, then it is up to us to decide whether to believe them or not. What is not up to us is the construction of our own creed on the basis of some preconceived ideas about the incompatibility of faith and miracle.

May I remark in passing that the rejection of miracle which is so basic to Bultmann's position smacks to me of that sort of antiseptic Christianity which is quite ready to admit that God may *speak* to us in the language which a Palestinian fisherman of the first century would understand but which will never allow that

God could be so incredibly vulgar as to *act* in a way a well-bred academic of the twentieth century would find distasteful. For if anything would have been incredible to first-century man it would have been a God who did no miracles.

To go on, however. In order to justify demythologizing, Bultmann must prove not only that the resurrection is an impossibility if taken literally, but also that the resurrection is actually a myth in the New Testament. He does so by two arguments: 1. The mythologies of the ancient world contain stories of dying and rising gods and we do not hesitate to call these myths; 2. The New Testament actually uses the resurrection as a myth, and this is the real purpose of its proclamation of the resurrection.

It is true that stories of dying and rising gods are known from ancient mythology. It is also true, and Bultmann neglects to mention this, that in the Judaism of the time of Christ there was a widespread belief in the resurrection of men. You have clear evidence of this belief, for example, in Daniel 12:2 and 2 Maccabees 12:43. Bultmann's own avowal that the New Testament often uses the resurrection as miraculous proof testifies also to this literal belief in the resurrection of the dead as something quite within God's power and to be expected in the last days. Therefore, that resurrection is a mythological theme in other literatures in no way proves that resurrection is ever mythological in the New Testament.

The text of 1 Corinthians 15 is extremely important in this regard. This epistle is one of the oldest pieces of the New Testament, and in chapter fifteen Paul appeals to an even older tradition, one which goes back to the original witnesses to the resurrection:

Now I would remind you, brethren, in what terms I

preached to you the gospel, which you received, in which
you stand, by which you are saved, if you hold it fast—
unless you believed in vain. For I delivered to you as
of first importance what I also received, that Christ died
for our sins in accordance with the scriptures, that he
was buried, that he was raised on the third day in accordance with the scriptures, and that he appeared to Cephas,
then to the twelve. Then he appeared to more than five
hundred brethren at one time, most of whom are still
alive, though some have fallen asleep. Then he appeared
to James, then to all the apostles. Last of all, as to one
untimely born, he appeared also to me. For I am the least
of the apostles, unfit to be called an apostle, because I
persecuted the church of God. But by the grace of God
I am what I am, and his grace toward me was not in
vain. On the contrary, I worked harder than any of them,
though it was not I, but the grace of God which is with
me. Whether then it was I or they, so we preach and
so you believed.[11]

It is not only that Paul appeals to witnesses who had
seen the risen Lord. It is not only that the phrase "he
was buried" is very difficult to explain apart from the
tradition of the empty tomb. It is the context in which
Paul appeals to the resurrection which shows us that
he takes it literally. He appeals to the resurrection of
Jesus in answer to those who were saying that the
dead do not rise.

If Christ has not been raised, your faith is futile and you
are still in your sins. Then those also who have fallen
asleep in Christ have perished. If it is for this life only
that we have put our hope in Christ, then we are the
most unhappy of men. But in fact Christ has been raised
from the dead, the first fruits of those who have fallen
asleep.[12]

In a comparable passage in 1 Thessalonians 4 there is
this same connection of the resurrection of Jesus with

the resurrection of those who have already died in the
Christian community:

We would not have you ignorant, brethren, concerning
those who are asleep, that you may not grieve as others
do who have no hope. For since we believe that Jesus
died and rose again, even so God will bring with him
those who have fallen asleep through Jesus.[13]

The hope for those who have died is in Jesus who
died too but rose from the dead. Could anything be
clearer? Paul is talking about the actual return from
the dead of the man Jesus of Nazareth. He knows
quite well the seriousness of what he is saying, for if
what he says is not true then "we are even found to
be misrepresenting God, because we testified of God
that he raised Christ, whom he did not raise if it is
true that the dead are not raised." [14]

While these passages from Paul's epistles are extremely important, they are not at all the only texts
which take the resurrection literally. All the accounts
of the discovery of the empty tomb do so. So too do
those accounts in the Gospels which tell of the risen
Christ taking food or showing His wounds to His
disciples. Bultmann recognizes this, after all, when he
admits that often the resurrection is used as a miraculous proof. Surely one must take the resurrection
literally in order to use it as a miraculous proof.

Therefore, at least some texts (in fact, all texts
which give an account of the resurrection) take it as
an actual fact, not as a myth. Bultmann must dismiss
these texts of the New Testament if he is to maintain
his view that the New Testament uses the resurrection
as a myth. He does so on the grounds that these texts
of the New Testament have misunderstood the real
purpose of the proclamation of the resurrection in the

first preaching. This real purpose was to proclaim the resurrection as the event of salvation. Bultmann understands by event of salvation that which actually offers me salvation now. Thus when I hear Christ preached as risen from the dead what makes this preaching a saving event for me is that I understand this event to be that which calls me to decision to accept the possibility of dying to my old self and rising to my new self.

It is evident that Bultmann is being faithful to the New Testament when he says that its real purpose in proclaiming the resurrection is in proclaiming it as the event of salvation. The resurrection of Jesus is not just something extraordinary that happened to a particular man in the past. It is an event upon which my salvation depends. At precisely this crucial point, though, Bultmann misunderstands the New Testament. He is entirely mistaken in supposing that he can separate the New Testament proclamation of the resurrection as the event of salvation from the proclamation that Jesus of Nazareth did really and truly come back from the tomb.

Let us again turn to St. Paul for light on this question. Bultmann finds in the epistles of Paul evidence of the correctness of his own position. He points to those texts which emphasize the "now" of salvation and the necessity of dying and rising with Christ in the present moment. These texts, in his opinion, prove that Paul is preaching the resurrection as the event of salvation by which God has actually intervened to offer man the possibility of new life. Only this is Paul interested in, not in the resurrection as miracle. This is to use the resurrection mythologically, however— to convey a new understanding of existence, and we are justified in not taking literally the resurrection of Jesus of Nazareth from the grave.

What shows most clearly how this view distorts the thought of Paul is to confront it with what breathes in every one of Paul's epistles—his deep personal attachment to his risen Lord. If Jesus is not risen from the dead, what do the following statements mean?

The love of Christ urges us on, because we are convinced that one has died for all; therefore, all have died. And he died for all, that those who live might live no longer for themselves but for him who for their sake died and was raised.[15]

I have been crucified with Christ; it is no longer I who live, but Christ who lives in me; and the life I now live in the flesh I live by faith in the Son of God who loved me and gave himself for me.[16]

Whatever gain I had, I counted as loss for the sake of Christ. Indeed I count everything as loss because of the surpassing worth of knowing Christ Jesus my Lord. For his sake I have suffered the loss of all things, and count them as refuse, in order that I may gain Christ and be found in him, not having a righteousness of my own, based on law, but that which is through faith in Christ, the righteousness from God that depends on faith; that I may know him and the power of his resurrection and may share his sufferings becoming like him in his death, that if possible I may attain the resurrection from the dead.[17]

For to me to live is Christ, and to die is gain. If it is to be life in the flesh, that means fruitful labor for me. Yet which I shall choose I cannot tell. I am hard pressed between the two. My desire is to depart and be with Christ, for that is far better.[18]

If I may say so, Paul has not realized the extent of his delusion. He is not only wrong about the resurrection of Jesus from the dead, but he has fallen in love with a myth. Bultmann's explanation of the resurrection makes Paul's love for Christ meaningless.

By demythologizing the resurrection, Bultmann has emptied the New Testament of what is its message, that salvation comes to us in and through the person of Jesus of Nazareth who is living now to make intercession for us as Lord and Christ. Bultmann takes no account of this present relationship between the believer and Jesus of Nazareth who is Lord. How can it be otherwise in a theory which makes so much of myth? If the Christian message is myth, then it is about human existence and the person of Christ is symbol of this meaning. The New Testament, on the contrary, is fundamentally about Jesus of Nazareth who *gives* meaning to human existence by His life, death, and resurrection.

The effort to make mythological truth the truth which saves just will not wash. The New Testament message is too much bound to the particular, to the historical. It deals with the unique, the once-for-all happening, and therefore, the truth of the New Testament and of its central proclamation of salvation is a truth much more closely related to history than to myth. New Testament history is a special kind of history to be sure, a history which is also a faith, a creed.

II

THE CREED AND THE NEW TESTAMENT

It is the truth which God willed to commit to sacred writing for the sake of our salvation which is the primary object of the interpreter's investigation of the New Testament. Those who would demythologize the New Testament claim by their method to arrive at this truth or, as they call it, the essential message of the New Testament. My objection to their claim is that they are mistaken in saying that myth is the mode in which that message is expressed. I say that the literary form in which the message of salvation is cast is much more akin to history than to myth, to history which is at the same time creed.

Let me begin to pursue that idea further by drawing attention to the traditional creeds by which the Church professes her faith. It is characteristic of these creeds that the central portion is devoted to a history of salvation; this, for example, is the way the creed recited at Sunday Mass does it:

And I believe in one Lord, Jesus Christ, the only-begotten Son of God, born of the Father before all ages, God of God, Light of Light, true God of true God, begotten not made, of one substance with the Father by whom all things were made, who for us men and for our salvation came down from heaven, and he became flesh by the Holy Spirit of the Virgin Mary, and was made man. He was also crucified for us, suffered under Pontius Pilate, and was buried, and on the third day he rose again, according to the Scriptures. He ascended into heaven and sits at the right hand of the Father. He will come again in glory to judge the living and the dead, and of his kingdom there will be no end.[19]

The beginning of this portion of the creed identifies the person involved in this history of salvation, the Son of God, and the end of the same passage changes from history to prophecy; but for the most part we have here statements about the past in which salvation was wrought by Jesus Christ. Now the Church has traditionally held that in these creeds she is expressing and professing the truth of salvation, and that this truth is the same as that which the New Testament proclaims.

Of course, if demythologizing works on the New Testament, it could work on the creeds as well. There is one difference, however. It is extremely difficult, not to say impossible, to maintain that the Church in using these creeds throughout the centuries to profess her faith has understood them in a mythological sense. She has rather understood them as making true statements about what was done by and in Jesus of Nazareth for our salvation. The Gnostic controversies of the second century made clear that the Church rejected an interpretation of her faith which would dissolve the ties binding it to the person of Jesus of Nazareth whom she worshiped as Lord. The demythologizers must simply claim that for centuries the Christian Church has erred by taking literally what in the primitive preaching of the New Testament was intended mythologically. Is this a valid claim? What foundation is there for the Church's conviction that her creeds really do contain the same faith, the same truth of salvation, which the New Testament proclaims? Let us look at the New Testament.

The one word which best describes its message is not "myth" but "gospel." It is the word traditionally used to name those four accounts of the life of Jesus which the Church recognizes as canonical. The epistles of Paul show us that the word "gospel" was in use to describe the New Testament message long before the Gospels as we know them were written: "Christ did not send me to baptize, but to preach the gospel." [20] Nor does Paul imagine himself different from the other apostles as preachers of the gospel. At the beginning of chapter fifteen of First Corinthians he writes, "Now

I would remind you, brethren, in what terms I preached to you the gospel, which you received, in which you stand, by which you are saved, if you hold it fast, unless you believed in vain." [21] Then after reminding them what that gospel was which he preached he concludes, "Whether then it was I or they, so we preach and so you believed." [22] Thus any attempt to determine the central message of the New Testament must begin with the gospel preached from the first.

What were the contents of the gospel which Paul and the others preached? Since we have just spoken of 1 Corinthians 15, let us begin with that text.

For I delivered to you as of first importance what I also received, that Christ died for our sins in accordance with the scriptures, that he was buried, that he was raised on the third day in accordance with the scriptures, and that he appeared to Cephas, then to the twelve. Then he appeared to more than five hundred brethren at one time, most of whom are still alive, though some have fallen asleep. Then he appeared to James, then to all the apostles. Last of all, as to one untimely born, he appeared also to me.[23]

The contents of the gospel in this text are the events of Christ's death, resurrection, and manifestation to or commissioning of witnesses to the resurrection; yet these events are related as something more than bare facts. Christ is said to have died "for our sins." Both His death and resurrection are said to be "in accordance with the scriptures." What we have here are the events of Christ's death and resurrection along with an interpretation of these events which reveals them to be of significance for us in fulfilment of the prophecies of the Old Testament. There is a further element of interpretation in this gospel which it is easy to overlook at first, the use of the title "Christ." This title expresses at one and the same time both the idea that these events are for our salvation and that they are fulfilment of prophecy, for the Christ, the Messiah, was He who was to come to deliver Israel. By applying this title to Jesus of Nazareth the gospel interprets the life of this Jesus who was crucified, and proclaims the meaning of that life for us.

Another text of Paul also gives a brief account of what the gospel is he preaches:

Paul, a servant of Jesus Christ, called to be an apostle, set apart for the gospel of God which he promised beforehand through his prophets in the holy scriptures, the gospel concerning his Son, who was descended from David according to the flesh and designated Son of God in power according to the Spirit of holiness by his resurrection from the dead, Jesus Christ our Lord, through whom we have received grace and apostleship to bring about obedience to the faith for the sake of his name among all the Gentiles, including yourselves who are called to belong to Jesus Christ.[24]

Here again is that same combination of fact and interpretation. This Jesus who died and rose from the dead is God's own Son who is Lord and Christ by His resurrection from the dead. He is the one God promised beforehand by the prophets.

The Acts of the Apostles is another important source for the contents of the gospel preached from the first. We are taken back by its author to the very beginnings of the gospel preaching, to the first Pentecost, and to the subsequent sermons of Peter in the early days in Jerusalem. If we allow for certain anachronisms introduced by Luke into his account of the earliest preaching, we can still see that it is basically the same gospel Paul preached. "Let all the house of

Israel therefore know assuredly that God has made
him both Lord and Christ, this Jesus whom you crucified," [25] Peter ends his first gospelling. You have in
these sermons of Acts the same combination of fact
and interpretation. This Jesus who died God has raised
from the dead to fulfil the scriptures in which He had
promised the Christ to Israel to save them from their
sins.

If we compare this gospel in Paul and in Acts to the
four Gospels we can see that the gospel preached from
the earliest days has carried through and imposed its
particular point of view, its particular interpretation,
upon these much longer accounts of the life, death,
and resurrection of Jesus. Thus, while we are told in
much more detail about the teaching and work of
Jesus in His public ministry, still that interpretation
of the events of His life which turns those events into
gospel remains the same. That is, this Jesus born of the
Virgin Mary, mighty in word and work, who suffered
under Pontius Pilate, was crucified, died, and was
buried, who rose again the third day, who appeared
to certain chosen witnesses is He who was promised
by God in the scriptures. He is Lord and Christ, and
it is through faith in Him that men are saved. Thus
gospel is central to the New Testament and what is
central to gospel is the interpretation of the life, death,
and resurrection of Jesus of Nazareth proposed to the
faith of those to whom the gospel is preached.

One cannot separate the facts from their interpretation. For example, one cannot separate the bodily
resurrection of Jesus from the interpretation that by
this resurrection Jesus is designated Lord and Christ
because it is precisely in the bodily resurrection of
Jesus that the interpretation of its significance is revealed. The resurrection of Jesus from the dead is,

indeed, the event which is interpreted as the event of salvation. Yet the meaning of the resurrection cannot be read from the event alone. That is why the resurrection is an article of faith. It is not that one accepts the bodily resurrection of Jesus as a fact and then concludes from this fact that Jesus is Lord and Christ. In this Bultmann is quite right. Rather it is that along with the sight of the risen Jesus is given to the chosen witnesses the revelation that He is Lord and Christ. It is this revelation, not the simple fact of the return to life of Jesus, which makes known to faith alone the uniqueness of His resurrection. Therefore, this gospel message is proposed to faith, and when it is accepted in faith it becomes creed; its articles relate the history of salvation in Jesus Christ.

If we would delve a little deeper into this type of creed and its antecedents, we must push our inquiry back into the Old Testament. Essential to this revealed interpretation of the events of Jesus' life is that "they fulfilled what God had promised beforehand by the prophets." These historical events then are themselves considered to be the culmination of a long history which led up to them. For this reason we cannot fully understand the historical character of the gospel message without understanding something of the faith of Israel.

The word "gospel" itself carries us back into the Old Testament. In 1 Peter we read:

You have been born anew, not of perishable seed but of imperishable, through the living and abiding word of God; for "All flesh is like grass and all its glory like the flower of grass. The grass withers, and the flower falls, but the word of the Lord abides forever." That word is the good news which was preached to you.[26]

Peter is quoting Isaiah 40:6–8, and he interprets the

word of God there referred to as the good news, the gospel, which was preached to Christians. This text of Isaiah does in fact continue in this way:

Get you up to a high mountain, O Zion, herald of good tidings; lift up your voice with strength, O Jerusalem, herald of good tidings, lift it up, fear not; say to the cities of Judah, Behold your God! Behold, the Lord God comes with might and his arm rules for him; behold, his reward is with him, and his recompense before him. He will feed his flock like a shepherd, he will gather the lambs in his arms, he will carry them in his bosom, and gently lead those that are with young.[27]

The "good tidings" this text describes are of the coming of the Lord. This hopeful message saw in the events which led to the return of Israel from her Babylonian exile the hand of God. Though He had abandoned them for a moment He had returned to them to save them. The gospel, or good tidings of salvation, answered the hopeful desire of the people for God's coming to them by announcing His approach to restore them. The people recognized Jesus as herald of these glad tidings when He came saying, "The time is fulfilled, and the kingdom of God is at hand; repent and believe in the good news [gospel]." [28]

The very word gospel used to describe the New Testament message announces the fulfilment of past hope. All the hopes raised by the prophetic heralds of good tidings in the Old Testament find fulfilment in the Christ who is the object of the gospel. As Paul puts it, it is "the gospel of God which he promised beforehand through his prophets in the holy scriptures." [29]

This Old Testament hope raised by many a prophetic voice was itself rooted in the faith of the people of Israel in a God who was their God and from whom

they could expect a future full of promise. This hope
of theirs was bolstered by the evidence of God's love
for them which they found in their past history. In
fact, if one would characterize Israelite faith in a few
words one could say that it was a faith in the God
who had loved them in the past and would never stop
loving them in the future. According to Israelite
faith, her history began when God revealed Himself
to Abraham. And when God reveals Himself to Moses
He identifies Himself as a God with a past. "I am the
God of Abraham, of Isaac, and of Jacob," He says.
Later, after the escape of the Israelites from Egypt,
God again identifies Himself to them by His past. "I
am Yahweh your God who brought you out of the
land of Egypt, out of the house of bondage." [30] So
important was their past history to their religion that
the Israelites recited that history as a creed. The following is a profession of faith made by the individual
son of Israel each time he brought his offering of first
fruits to the place of worship:

A wandering Aramean was my father; and he went down
into Egypt and sojourned there, few in number; and there
he became a nation, great, mighty, and populous. And
the Egyptians treated us harshly, and afflicted us, and laid
upon us hard bondage. Then we cried to the Lord the
God of our fathers, and the Lord heard our voice, and
saw our affliction, our toil, and our oppression; and the
Lord brought us out of Egypt with a mighty hand and
an outstretched arm, with great terror, with signs and
wonders; and he brought us into this place and gave us
this land, a land flowing with milk and honey. And behold
now I bring the first of the fruit of the ground, which
thou, O Lord, hast given me.[31]

This profession of faith has for its articles the past
history of Israel, but this history is no ordinary history.

According to their belief their history was guided by God for a definite purpose which was to lead them into a land flowing with milk and honey where they might render Him the tribute of their worship in gratitude. Just as we have seen with regard to the gospel, so too in the Old Testament the faith is expressed in an historical creed dealing with the salvation God had wrought on their behalf.

Moreover, this historical creed was not something peripheral to Old Testament religion. As the German scholar Gerhard von Rad has shown, this type of creed provided the format according to which the first six books of the Bible were organized.[32] Thus these books with all their various traditions and sources find their unity in the faith of a people in the God who has acted on their behalf in the past.

From another point of view as well, recent studies have shown the central place of this historical creed in the religion of Israel. It has been shown that an essential part of the covenant which made Israel the people of God was devoted to a recital of the past favours granted Israel by God. In Exodus 20:1 as a prelude to the Ten Commandments God identifies Himself as the God who delivered the people from Egypt. In Josue 24 in connection with the renewal of the covenant a much longer recital of the favours God has granted in the past precedes the consent of the people to be a party to the pact with God.

It is extremely interesting to note that the literary form which may have served as model for the Israelite covenant is not found in mythological texts of other peoples but in treaties made between king and vassal 1500 years before Christ. In these treaties an historical part is found which describes the history of the relationship between the two kingdoms with special refer-

ence to the favors bestowed on the vassal by his overlord. The legal purpose of this history seems to be to
establish the legal right of the overlord to his vassal's
fealty. It is meant to stir the latter to gratitude as well.
As far as can be determined, the history itself is not
exaggerated fantasy, but adheres fairly well to the
actual facts of the past.[33]

It is certainly of some importance that the closest
parallels found to something so central to Israel's religion as the covenant are found, not in the mythologies of the time, but in treaties in which history
really matters because the past is essential to that which
determines the present relationship of the contracting
parties. All forms of language fail when they must
represent a relationship in which one partner is God.
Yet it is of the greatest importance to interpretation
to know what forms of speech the Old Testament
actually uses to express its faith. One cannot escape
the fact that the faith of Israel is cast in a form of
history and not of myth. To apply to this form of
history canons proper to the interpretation of myth
is to make of the faith of Israel something it is not.

The God of Israel was not a God of the past only,
however. He was the God of the present and of the
future. By what He had done in the past He founded
His right to demand obedience of His people in the
present. Just as He had been their God in the past,
and they had been His people, so in the present was
He their God and they *must* be His people. The present demand, as we have seen, was all of a piece with
the past history of the people.

God was also a God of promise for the future. The
prophets most prominently held out this hope to the
people, though the promise of future blessing was also
part of the covenant. The point I wish to emphasize

with regard to the hope of Israel is that the prophets draw upon the past history of the people rather than upon mythology for the images and words in which they announce this hope of the future. The exodus from Egypt, the wandering in the desert, the entrance into the promised land, the temple, the covenant, Jerusalem—all these become for the prophets symbols of the new salvation God is preparing for His people. So too the great men of their past who were the mediators of God's salvation to them become symbols of the One who is to come. Especially David the king and his line as inheritors of God's promise of perpetual kingship serve the hope of the coming Christ. Other figures play a role as well. Moses promised that God would raise up a prophet like to Himself. The prophets of the past themselves become figures in this future hope. As servants and messengers who speak in God's name and often suffer for so speaking they are used by the prophet of Isaiah 40–55 as the material from which he draws the majestic portrait of the Suffering Servant of Yahweh. The object of this hope was, then, very much in word and image conceived of as a part of that history of which He was the culmination.

Yet as it turned out and as the gospel announced it He was much more than had been expected. He was God's only Son. He came down from heaven, the Word of God who was God and was made flesh. Here, at least, you might say, the language of the gospel is the language of myth. But that would be too hasty a conclusion. Even the most exalted titles of Jesus can be found in an historical context in the Old Testament. Son of God, for example, was a title applied to Israel, and referred to the special status of the people of God. So too the kings of the Davidic line were addressed as son of God to signify the legitimacy of their claim to the throne as it depended upon divine election. The king was even addressed as lord in the court usage of the day as were lesser notables.

These titles are given new meaning in the New Testament, not so much because they are given the meaning they might have in contemporary myths, but because Jesus of Nazareth is hailed not simply as the last in a long line of mediators of God's salvation; He is hailed as the *divine partner* in that history as well. That history of Israel which was its faith was the history of the relationship between God and His people. These two partners made that history together. As Deuteronomy says, "What great nation is there that has a god so near to it as the Lord our God is to us, whenever we call upon him?"[34] When God did do some new great act for His people it was said that God had visited His people or that they had seen His glory. So too was the word of God recognized as a power which served Him in all His works. The gospel simply states that that word which was the power of God for salvation was Jesus Emmanuel, God with us. The divine partner in the history of salvation has entered history in a new way by becoming man.

Thus one need not look to mythology to understand the gospel of Jesus Christ. The language of the gospel can only properly be understood as the reality of Jesus' identity at work upon the language of the sacred history of Israel. The God of ages past acted once more by sending His Son as bearer of salvation. Of course, there are those for whom the telling argument in favor of a mythological explanation is simply that the incarnation just could not possibly be true in the sense in which it has been understood in the past.

They should, however, admit that they are then not interpreting but disagreeing with the Paul who wrote, "When the time had fully come, God sent forth his Son, born of woman, born under the Law, to redeem those who were under the law, so that we might receive adoption as sons." [35]

Now, I have stressed that the gospel gives an interpretation of the events of Jesus' life which is addressed to faith alone. It is a revelation of the meaning of those events. In the Epistle to the Galatians Paul talks about where this revelation came from:

I would have you know, brethren, that the gospel which was preached by me is not man's gospel. For I did not receive it from man, nor was I taught it, but it came through a revelation of Jesus Christ. For you have heard of my former life in Judaism, how I persecuted the church of God violently and tried to destroy it; and I advanced in Judaism beyond many of my own age among my people, so extremely zealous was I for the traditions of my fathers. But when he who had set me apart before I was born, and had called me through his grace was pleased to reveal his Son in me, in order that I might preach him among the Gentiles, I did not confer with flesh and blood, nor did I go up to Jerusalem to those who were apostles before me, but I went away into Arabia; and again I returned to Damascus.[36]

God is the one who reveals His Son in Paul, and we know from comparing this text with others such as 1 Corinthians 15:8 that this revelation came to Paul when Christ appeared to him. Along with this revelation came the commission to preach the gospel. Notice the connection of apostleship and sight of the risen Lord: "Am I not free? Am I not an apostle? Have I not seen Jesus our Lord?" [37] In Romans, after describing the gospel he preaches, Paul says of Jesus Christ that it was through Him that "we have received grace and apostleship to bring about obedience to the faith for the sake of his name among all the Gentiles." [38] Thus according to Paul it was through the revelation of the gospel to him by the risen Christ that he received his commission to preach.

What of the other apostles? How did they learn their gospel, that combination of fact and interpretation which proclaimed Jesus to be Lord and Christ, the fulfilment of the promise of salvation? According to the tradition found in 1 Corinthians 15, what qualifies all of the gospel preachers is their having seen the risen Christ. It is difficult to determine just how much of the meaning and the purpose of His life Jesus revealed even to His disciples during His public ministry. The Gospels give us the distinct impression that even His closest followers, while finally taking Him for the Christ, were usually in a state of perplexity about what it all meant. Certainly it is true that the crucifixion came as a sudden shock to all the hopes they had been building up around Him.

The Gospels of Matthew and Luke testify most explicitly that it was from the *risen* Christ that the apostles received the true meaning of the events they witnessed:

All power has been given to me in heaven and on earth. Go therefore and make disciples of all nations, baptizing them in the name of the Father and of the Son and of the Holy Spirit, teaching them to observe all that I have commanded you; and behold I am with you always, to the end of the world.[39]

Thus does the risen Christ according to Matthew reveal His Lordship and commission His disciples to bring to Him all the nations.

In Luke's Gospel it is the risen Christ who explains the meaning of His death and resurrection by interpreting to the disciples the scriptures:

These are my words which I spoke to you while I was still with you, that everything written about me in the law of Moses and the prophets and the psalms must be fulfilled. Then he opened their minds to understand the scriptures, and said to them, Thus it is written, that the Christ should suffer and on the third day rise from the dead, and that repentance and forgiveness of sins should be preached in his name to all nations.[40]

In all the Gospels this revelation Jesus makes to His disciples begins in the public ministry. We may suspect that the understanding which came with the revelation of the Lord after His resurrection has influenced this telling of the public ministry. At all events, what is clear is that the New Testament knows only one answer to the question of the origin of the gospel interpretation of the life, death, and resurrection of Jesus. That answer is that Jesus Himself is the origin, especially the risen Jesus. It is His revelation of Himself that the apostles preach when they preach the gospel, and it is this same revelation that the Father confirmed by raising Jesus from the dead. Thus faith in the gospel of Jesus Christ is faith in Jesus of Nazareth, that Jewish son of a carpenter, who has revealed Himself to us and in so doing has revealed His Father also.

Gospel, then, is what we have been examining in this section. It is the central message of the New Testament, and what is characteristic of gospel is the announcement that Jesus of Nazareth has fulfilled the promises of salvation which God made to Israel, and He has done so by raising His Son from the dead. It is the proclamation that Jesus is Lord and Christ. I repeat: it is the proclamation that Jesus, this Jesus from Nazareth, is Lord and Christ. It is fully historical in this sense. Yet it is only by revelation that it can be known who Jesus really is and what the true meaning of His life is. Only by faith can this revelation be accepted. We have no access to this truth except through the word of Him who was raised from the dead. This faith is solidly grounded in the faith of Israel in the power of a God who has acted at particular moments in history according to a plan for His people. The gospel brings to fruition that plan and that revelation of God in history. Let us again listen to the credal formula with which we began this section:

I believe in one Lord, Jesus Christ, the only-begotten Son of God, born of the Father before all ages, God of God, Light of Light, true God of true God, begotten not made, of one substance with the Father by whom all things were made, who for us men and for our salvation came down from heaven, and he became flesh by the Holy Spirit of the Virgin Mary, and was made man. He was also crucified for us, suffered under Pontius Pilate, and was buried, and on the third day he rose again, according to the Scriptures. He ascended into heaven and sits at the right hand of the Father. He will come again in glory to judge the living and the dead, and of his kingdom there will be no end.[41]

The same faith which formulated this creed proclaimed the gospel. The creed can no more change than can the gospel because both propose to our faith what has happened once and for all. The creed has the same irreversibility as the past. It is not primarily the expression of a theological understanding of God and of man; neither is the gospel. That is why myth can never cope with gospel. Myth takes the Christian gospel, dissolves its ties with the particular, and produces the gnostic gospel of the Heavenly Man. Bultmann, who sees this difficulty, tries to solve it by a totally unwarranted appeal to a notion of *sola fide* to justify his belief *that* salvation has been offered to man while he maintains that this salvation has no more than an accidental connection with Jesus of Nazareth. On the contrary, the Christian gospel is nothing if it is not the gospel of Jesus of Nazareth through whom God acted in a certain definite way at a particular time and place, who was made Lord and Christ so that He is now the Way of all men to God. There's the rub, the scandal for modern man. One Jew who lived two thousand years ago is our Saviour today. Because of what He did then He is what He is today, living and reigning as our Lord. For this reason sound interpretation of the New Testament must always keep a firm grasp on the historical character of the faith according to which it was written, if that interpretation would succeed in understanding the truth God willed to commit to the scriptures for the sake of our salvation.

The gospel's history of salvation finds its faithful expression in the creed as traditionally understood. This is to say that the truth which God willed put into the scriptures for the sake of our salvation has been correctly understood and expressed in the creed —at least, that element of the truth of salvation which we have been talking about. (I have no intention of limiting the extent of the truth of salvation to this history of salvation. The future hope expressed both in New Testament and creed has been entirely passed over in our investigation.)

Now, it has been traditionally accepted that the creed faithfully expresses the gospel message of the history of our salvation—not because the creed was the product of any particularly eminent theologian, but because the creed was approved and taught by the Church as a true expression of her faith. To challenge the creed's interpretation of the gospel by another interpretation which would substantially alter our understanding of the gospel message is to challenge not just the creed but the Church as well who has guaranteed that creed by her authority.

As a matter of fact it should come as no surprise to anyone that conflicting interpretations of the New Testament are invariably accompanied by conflicting ideas about the Church and such Church-related questions as the canon, the authority, and the divine inspiration of the New Testament. These conflicts do not show up so clearly when interpreters limit themselves to the sense of any particular part of the New Testament. When once, however, the interpreter addresses himself to the truth which is for our salvation, to what we must believe and do *now* to be saved, then he is meeting the Church on her own ground, and it is there that battle lines are more sharply drawn.

III
THE CHURCH AND THE NEW TESTAMENT

Very much of the disagreement about the relationship of the Church to the New Testament can be traced to different interpretations of the meaning and normative value of the beginnings of Christianity and of the apostolic age for the post-apostolic Church. To illustrate this point and to introduce us to the question of the meaning of the apostolic age for the Church, I wish to outline what I consider to be a characteristic modern position with regard to the beginnings of Christianity and then to compare this position with what we know of the apostolic age from the New Testament. I hope, in doing so, to indicate the relationship which exists between the Church and New Testament at least with regard to certain essential features of the New Testament Church.

Let us begin with that particular interpretation of the beginnings of Christianity I referred to above. Christianity, it says, begins when the gospel of Jesus Christ is first preached, and when it finds its first believers. It is the word of God which, when accepted, calls men together as believers in Christ. What characterized these followers of the word as a community of believers was their belief that Christ was coming soon to found the kingdom of God and to usher in the end of the world. There was no question of a Church in the way we have come to understand it. First of all, there just was not time for the institution of a Church. The end was very near. Second, the earliest believers in Jesus, all of them Jews, thought of themselves not as forming a Church, but rather as the first fruits of the conversion of Israel or at least as that holy remnant of Israel which would be saved at the end of the world. There was a "Church" only in the very basic sense of the word, in the sense that the believers had been "called together" all of them by God's word and their response to it in humble faith.

Now this expectation was disappointed because Jesus did not come from heaven, and the world did not come to a speedy end. The believers were rather persecuted by their own countrymen, and at the same time the gospel received a hearing in the pagan world around them. These two factors, the delay of Christ's coming and the pagan acceptance–Jewish rejection of the gospel, combined to give the believers in Christ an identity of their own apart from Judaism. Especially did the delay of Christ's coming stimulate them to organize a Church which would preserve the gospel for a future of indefinite length. This change from expectation of kingdom to establishment of Church represented a substantial change in the form of community which incarnated the gospel. It took the whole first century and most of the second for this development to take place, and there was nothing sacrosanct about it. It was simply a response to the changing perspectives forced upon Christians by their awareness of their identity and of the lengthening distance between them and the end of the world. How can this form of the Christian Church claim exclusive divine origin when it is not even the most primitive form of the Christian Church? Just as the Catholic form of the Christian Church was born of the particular circumstances which accompanied the spread of the gospel in the first century, so can other forms be born of changing circumstances.

Christianity is not tied to any one of these ecclesiastical forms which happen to incarnate the essential message of the gospel. This message may be variously described as the fatherhood of God and the brotherhood of man, or the offer of the possibility of a new life, or that people matter, and so forth. In any case it is not one form of Church which is part of that essential message. It is usual at this point to utter an incantation which invokes the Holy Spirit and the freedom of the sons of God.

This is a challenging position and, I think, of more than passing interest today. Its reconstruction of the history of primitive Christianity is right at many points and is an improvement over the very simple view that the apostolic age saw no development in the Church at all. It is quite true that the earliest believers in Jesus did not think of themselves as forming a Church in the sense in which we know it, having

an identity and a future of its own apart from Israel.
In those early days before even the name "Christian"
had been applied to them, the believers looked upon
themselves as the beginning of the conversion of Israel,
and they expected the whole people to follow them.
As Peter is quoted as saying:

What God had foretold through the mouth of all the
prophets, namely, that his Christ should suffer, he has
fulfilled in the manner I have just described. Repent,
therefore, and be converted to have your sins taken away
so that the times of refreshment may come from the
presence of the Lord and he may send the Christ he has
foreordained for you, Jesus, whom the heavens must
receive till the time to set all things right, the time which
God promised long ago through the mouth of his holy
prophets.[42]

It is also true that certain circumstances which may
be described as fortuitous—that is, persecution by the
Jews and acceptance of the gospel by pagans, along
with the delay of the end of the world—stimulated
the development of the Church which by the end of
the New Testament period is already recognizably
Catholic.

To have discerned the development which went on
in the apostolic age is one of the important contribu-
tions modern Biblical study has made to interpretation
of the New Testament and to the treatise on the
Church in theology. It has forced theologians and
Biblicists alike to abandon the oversimplication which
imagined that Jesus revealed everything to the apostles
before He left them and that early Church history was
only a history of the apostles' successes and failures
as teachers to get all their knowledge to their disciples.

This, however, just brings us to the threshold of
the crucial issue. If we admit a real development in

the doctrine and life of the Church in the apostolic age, a progressive revelation as it is often called, we are still faced with alternative ways of understanding the apostolic age and of accounting for its normative value to the post-apostolic Church. For the sort of position outlined above, what is normative in the apostolic age, as far as I can gather, is the Word of God as it is authentically found in the most primitive preaching. There is here almost a mystical attraction exercised by the most primitive gospel. If we can get back to what the apostles preached on that first Easter Sunday, on that first Pentecost, then we have reached the authentic Word of God. What is most primitive is most pure Christianity, is most true, is closest to the source of the original inspiration of Christianity. It is interesting to note that the position which has most stressed development in the early Church is most afraid of development because development is corruption; it is straying from the garden of primeval innocence. Here you find all those appeals to the "earliest stratum" of the Gospels as to something of awe-inspiring holiness.

This is not the only way of looking at what is normative in the apostolic age. There is the Catholic position which, though it now is prepared to see much more development in the apostolic age, still looks upon this entire age as the *formative stage* of the Church. The apostolic work is conceived of more broadly as the founding of the Church, and that work was not completed until death put an end to their special apostolic gifts. It is not as though the apostles preached and then went away and hid from those they had preached to, so that the primitive preaching might retain its force. The apostles presided over the developments their preaching had begun. This in fact is where the New Testament supports the Catholic view. The development of the early Church did not just happen. It was initiated, directed, and presided over by the Lord Jesus, by His Spirit, and by the apostles, in order that the post-apostolic Church might be outfitted with what was essential for its continued life.

Let us look into this matter in more detail. The first observation I wish to make is this: it is a mistake to exaggerate the discontinuity between the most primitive community and its hope for the kingdom to come and the Church community which grew out of it. There are certain very important elements which remain constant through the change. The community began in the preaching of the gospel of Jesus Christ. We have seen that this gospel hailed Jesus as Lord and Christ. Therefore, it is not true to say that even the earliest community looked to a kingdom which was entirely in the future. By calling Jesus Lord and Christ the believer professed his faith that the kingdom of God had already begun, since Jesus had been enthroned at the right hand of God. The Psalm which the early preachers consistently applied to Jesus says, "The Lord said to my Lord: Sit at my right hand till I make your enemies your footstool." [43] The kingdom of Jesus the Christ has already begun in those who acknowledge Him as Lord.

It is wrong to write the history of primitive Christianity as though the Church took the place of the kingdom in the thinking of the first believers because their hopes had been disappointed. Faith in the kingdom already established in Christ remains an *unchanging* perspective and a guiding force in the development of the Church. Those who believe in Christ are already in His kingdom, yet they await His kingdom. This does not change. There is a lengthening of perspective

in that the first Christians begin to realize that the
return of Jesus is not going to come in their lifetime.
(What is of most special importance is when the apostles begin to realize this and reflect upon it; we will
return to this question.) However, it is precisely a
lengthening of perspective and not a change of perspective because the temporal element in the future
hope is completely secondary, and of little importance
within the perspective of the Lordship of Christ. This
is aptly illustrated by a text of Paul which at an early
date can completely describe the stages in the establishment of the kingdom without a single reference
to time.

But in fact Christ has been raised from the dead, the
first fruits of those who sleep. For as by a man came
death, by a man also has come resurrection from the dead.
For as in Adam all die, so also in Christ shall all be
made alive. But each in his own order; Christ the first
fruits, then at his coming those who belong to Christ.
Then comes the end, when he delivers the kingdom to
God the Father after destroying every rule and every
authority and power. For he must reign until he has put
all his enemies under his feet. The last enemy to be
destroyed is death. For God has put all things in subjection under his feet. But when it says, All things are put
in subjection under him, it is plain that exception is
made for him who is doing the subjecting. When all
things are subjected to him, then the Son himself will
also be subjected to him who put all things under him
that God may be everything to everyone.[44]

You can see by this text how Jesus as Lord now reigning spans all of future history and how that entire
history, no matter how long or how short, is subject
to the Lord enthroned in glory to whom all things
are being made subject. If he is Lord He has a king-

dom. Yet all His subjects have not yet been made part
of that kingdom. In this sense then Church never suc-
ceeds to kingdom. They exist at the same time in function of one another.

This community which knew Jesus as Lord was also
the community which had received the Spirit of God.
Peter, addressing the crowd at Pentecost, begins by
citing Joel the Prophet who foretold the outpouring of
the Spirit in the last days. The presence of the Spirit
in the community is taken for granted in all the letters
of Paul, even the earliest. Thus the Christian community is not only ruled by its Lord Jesus, but it is con-
fident of the inspiration of the Holy Spirit.

It is a community one enters by believing the gospel
and by being baptized in the name of the Lord Jesus.
It has its sacred meal in which the body and blood of
the Lord are eaten and drunk in memory of Him.
On the night before He suffered their Lord had given
them His blood which He called the blood of the covenant, and His people understood after His resurrection
that they had entered into the new covenant promised
for the last days by Jeremiah the Prophet. At one time
it was customary to attribute these rituals to pagan
influence which began to transform the early community into a Church. This position is much more
difficult to maintain today in the face of the evidence
from Qumran that analogous rites were practiced by
a Jewish sect itself thoroughly permeated by the expectation of the speedy end of all things. Certainly
no Biblical source informs us of a time when the Christian community did not practise baptism and celebrate
the Eucharist.

All these things characterized the Christian community from the beginning. It knew its Lord to be
enthroned as king at God's right hand. It knew the

Spirit to be in its midst. New believers were admitted to the community by baptism, and they celebrated the new covenant of which they were a part by the partaking of the body and blood of their Lord. As the community developed, all these factors were constants which persisted through the changing circumstances to preserve the identity of the developing community with the primitive community, and to preserve the unity among the many new communities being formed.

There is one constant in this early development of the Church which we have not yet touched upon, and it deserves special attention—the apostles. The Christian community was founded by men sent by Christ to preach the gospel. St. Paul writes:

Everyone who calls upon the name of the Lord will be saved. But how are men to call upon him in whom they have not believed? And how are they to believe in him of whom they have never heard? And how are they to hear without a preacher? And how can men preach unless they are sent? [45]

One cannot talk about the gospel without talking about those sent to preach the gospel. The word "apostle" means one-who-is-sent. We think first of all of the twelve, those who had been with Jesus during His public ministry and had been chosen by Him to be associated with His work. In this group Peter, the rock, has his place as leader. During the public ministry of Jesus their work was not primarily that of preaching, though they did some of that. They were disciples, learners in the school of Jesus. It is only after the resurrection that Jesus gives them their commission, that He sends them to preach His gospel. In full consciousness of the authority they have from the risen Lord to preach they do so.

Yet though the twelve form a special group within the early community there are others as well who are apostles. There is Paul, for instance, and there are those mentioned in 1 Corinthians 15:7 as witnesses to the resurrection. Indeed, the qualification to be apostle seems to have been precisely this witnessing of the resurrection and the commission to testify to the resurrection of Jesus.

Now what is of special importance is this: the apostles do not vanish from the scene immediately after the community is formed by their preaching; they remain as guides in the whole development of the early Church. By virtue of their calling and of the firsthand character of their witness to Jesus they teach the gospel of salvation with authority. Nowhere does the importance of this apostolic authority in the early Church appear more clearly than in the epistles of Paul. Often in disputes Paul must insist that his authority is no less than that of the other apostles. He thereby shows how fundamental that apostolic authority was in settling questions in the early Church. As he writes:

God has appointed in the church first apostles, second prophets, third teachers, then workers of miracles, then healers, helpers, administrators, speakers in various kinds of tongues.[46]

In this text the apostolic office is attributed to God's appointment. Other texts attribute their authority to the Spirit who is with them and who speaks through them.

Now we have received not the spirit of the world but the Spirit which is from God, that we might understand the gifts bestowed on us by God. And we impart this in words not taught by human wisdom but taught by the

Spirit, interpreting spiritual things to those who possess the Spirit.[47]

The prophets who prophesied of the grace that was to be yours searched and inquired about this salvation; they inquired what person or time was indicated by the Spirit of Christ within them when predicting the sufferings of Christ and the subsequent glory. It was revealed to them that they were serving not themselves but you, in the things which have now been announced to you by those who preached the gospel to you through the Holy Spirit sent from heaven, things into which angels long to look.[48]

Now the special apostolic office and authority means that the development of the Church in their time did not just happen. The early Church was moulded by the men to whom it was committed by Jesus Christ. It was their charge to see that that Church corresponded at every point to what their Lord intended.

The most instructive example of the way the apostolic authority worked in the growth of the early Church is the resolution of the question of the Gentiles' entry into the Church. If we are to take the Acts of the Apostles seriously, we must admit that the apostles did not at first understand that the gospel was for the Gentiles—at least not until Israel had been converted. It took a vision to Peter to reveal to him that the Gentiles were to be evangelized and baptized into the Church. Whether, in actual fact, the evangelization of the Gentiles had waited upon this vision of Peter recounted in Acts 10 or not, at least the apostles are there to judge this new development, to determine whether it is of the Holy Spirit, and to make authoritative decisions.

Paul recalls the same situation when the Gentiles were first entering the Church in Galatians 2:1–11. He disputes some of the practices of the Church lead-

ers because they are discriminatory against the Gentiles. He insists that his own authority is equal to that
of the other apostles, for he too has that authority directly from Jesus. Yet he understands the importance
of apostolic judgment. He describes his conversion
and his subsequent activity. He continues:

> Then after fourteen years I went up again to Jerusalem
> with Barnabas, taking Titus along with me. I went up by
> revelation; and I laid before them (but privately before
> those who were of repute) the gospel which I preach
> among the Gentiles lest somehow I should be running or
> had run in vain.[49]

A few lines later he says:

> And from those who were reputed to be something (what
> they were makes no difference to me; God shows no par-
> tiality)—those, I say, who were of repute added nothing
> to me; but on the contrary, when they saw that I had
> been entrusted with the gospel to the uncircumcised, just
> as Peter had been entrusted with the gospel to the cir-
> cumcised (for he who worked through Peter for the
> mission to the circumcised worked through me also for
> the Gentiles), and when they perceived the grace that
> was given to me, James and Cephas and John, who were
> reputed to be pillars, gave to me and Barnabas the right
> hand of fellowship, that we should go to the Gentiles
> and they to the circumcised; only they would have us
> remember the poor, which very thing I was eager to do.[50]

This handling of the Gentiles' entry into the Church
can teach us two things. First, the authority of the
apostles does not mean they do everything themselves,
initiate every new development. There is a keen sense
in the early Church that the Spirit is at work in all
believers. The first apostles learn from Paul, but they
also learn from what the Holy Spirit does in the Christian community. Peter's reaction to the conversion of

the household of Cornelius as recounted in Acts 10:44–48 is illustrative of this point. On the other hand—and this is the second thing the case of the Gentiles teaches us—this new development does not take place apart from the exercise of apostolic supervision. The apostles are convinced that they have the authority to decide the question because they hold their commission from the Lord and because they have the Spirit of God.

This is consistent with the picture of the early Church which we have from the epistles of the New Testament. The various communities do not grow up in isolation from one another. Paul writes to the churches he has founded, but he also confers with those who were apostles before him in Jerusalem and he retains close ties with the church at Antioch which first sponsored his missionary activity (according to Acts 13:1–3). The Epistle to the Romans shows Paul in communication with another church which was not founded by him but which was the object of his zeal to fulfil his mandate as apostle to teach and deepen the faith of fellow believers. The rest of the epistolary literature reflects this same apostolic concern.

Writing was not the only means which Paul made use of to exercise his apostolic mandate at a distance. We learn from his letters that he sent his personal representatives to visit and sometimes to restore order in the churches he founded. We know, for example, of Timothy's mission to the Thessalonian church from 1 Thessalonians 3:1–5 and of the mission of Titus to the Corinthian church from 2 Corinthians 7:5–16. Thus to present the Christian communities of these early days as unstructured groups gathered together to hear the word of the gospel and to celebrate the fellowship of charity is to create a false impression by not telling the whole story. The picture painted by this view neglects the apostles. It completely ignores the fact that they were a *continuing* force throughout the early years of Church history. Perhaps it would be more true to say that the apostles in this view are treated as though apostleship were not permanently theirs or that the authority they received from Christ to preach the gospel did not extend to the preservation and fostering of the right understanding and development of that gospel in the lives of those who had believed through them. What is most evident in the New Testament, however, is that those who were apostles by Christ's appointment and witnesses to His resurrection were permanently apostles. Therefore, the apostolic work must be taken in its entirety, as a finished product. It is their lives' work and that work is the Church which they were founding and guiding through its formative stage. From this perspective, to consider that the earliest apostolic work is somehow the best, the most free from corruption or from the human element, is simply a mistake.

If we adopt the view that the apostolic age must be viewed as a unity as the apostolic work, then we can see too why it has a unique normative value for the post-apostolic Church. The apostles are irreplaceable; they had seen and heard Jesus, had been His disciples, and most especially had witnessed His resurrection. There can be no more apostles in the Church. We all of us receive at second hand what they received firsthand. Therefore, there is no authority in the post-apostolic Church which can equal theirs.

Yet what they left to succeeding generations was not the dead weight of memoirs cast in bronze but a living Church. Their work must not be looked upon as a whole only in the temporal sense, unfinished until death stilled their voices; it must also be looked upon as a whole in its extension to every area of Church life. The Second Vatican Council describes the apostolic tradition in this way:

Now what was handed on by the apostles includes everything which contributes to the holiness of life, and the increase in faith of the People of God; and so the Church, in her teaching, life, and worship, perpetuates and hands on to all generations all that she herself is, all that she believes.[51]

The New Testament records only a small portion of the immense activity and influence of the apostles on the early Church, yet the Acts and the epistles of Paul give us glimpses enough of it to convince us of its reality and importance. The Church in all its aspects as it emerges from the apostolic age must be acknowledged to be the work of the apostles.

Of course, the teaching of the apostles, their gospel, is a most substantial part of their legacy to the post-apostolic Church. Except for Paul, whose literary activity was immense, the apostles themselves do not seem to have left much of a written record of their teaching. It was left to their associates and disciples to preserve their gospel in this way. Luke makes this point clear in the prologue he writes to his Gospel:

Inasmuch as many have undertaken to compile a narrative of the things which have been accomplished among us, just as they were delivered to us by those who from the beginning were eyewitnesses and ministers of the word, it seemed good to me also, having followed all things closely for some time past, to write an orderly account for you, most excellent Theophilus, that you may know the truth concerning the things of which you have been informed.[52]

The collection of writings which became the New Testament is the product of this desire to preserve the teaching of the apostles for the post-apostolic Church.

The New Testament itself, however, testifies that the concern of the apostles to preserve the gospel free from error when they began to contemplate their own passing was not primarily with the writing-down of the gospel. Rather it was with those who would carry on the teaching role in the Church after the apostles. First and Second Timothy along with the Epistle to Titus are filled with exhortations for the teacher that he be faithful to the sound doctrine learned from the apostles. There are warnings against false teachers and admonitions to guard the deposit of faith. First Peter 5:1–11 with its exhortation to the elders of the churches of Asia reflects the same apostolic concern. Perhaps the most moving account of this apostolic concern comes from the pen of Luke when he gives us Paul's farewell address to the elders of the church at Ephesus. I quote a portion of it.

And now, behold, I know that all you among whom I have gone about preaching the kingdom will see my face no more. Therefore I testify to you this day that I am innocent of the blood of all of you, for I did not shrink from declaring to you the whole counsel of God. Take heed to yourselves and to all the flock, in which the Holy Spirit has made you guardians, to feed the church of the Lord which he obtained with his own blood. I know that after my departure fierce wolves will come in among you, not sparing the flock; and from among your own selves will arise men speaking perverse things, to draw away the disciples after them. Therefore, be alert, remembering that for three years I did not cease night or day to admonish every one with tears. And now

I commend you to God and to the word of his grace, which is able to build you up and to give you the inheritance among all those who are sanctified.[53]

The basic idea behind the apostolic succession in the Church is very simply that this pastoral care first exercised by the apostles with divine assistance and authority continues in the Church. It is, in a way, the finishing touch the apostles put to the work God had given them to do. They left to the Church they had founded not only the gospel they had preached but the authority necessary to continue that preaching and to preserve that gospel free from error to succeeding generations. Thus does the Church, especially through those who have had committed to them the pastoral care, the bishops and the pope, claim to be the authentic interpreter of the New Testament insofar as she continues to teach with divine assistance the truth which God willed put into Sacred Writ for the sake of our salvation.

At the beginning of these pages on New Testament interpretation I said that my intent was not to propose a new interpretation; rather it was to provide some criteria for judging the validity of new interpretations. We have seen that gospel is the fundamental form in which the New Testament message was cast, and that history occupies a place in gospel which it could never occupy in myth. The relationship between New Testament and Church shows an inner unity between the truth which is for salvation and the authority to teach that truth; this is seen in the role which the apostles played in the founding of the Church. The divinely appointed apostolic work must be looked upon as a unity, as the guiding of the Church through her formative stage, rather than as simply the primitive preaching of the gospel. Looked at in this light, the apostles' manifest concern for the continuation of their teaching mission after they had gone is the finishing touch on their work. The role of the Church as interpreter of Scripture is, then, part of her legacy from the apostles.

If what I have said is true, then a general principle may be stated for judging the validity of interpretations of the New Testament. Any new interpretation must be consistent, first with the historical character of the gospel and the Christian faith, especially as it bears upon the person and work of Jesus of Nazareth; second with the Church's understanding of the truth of the New Testament as expressed in her authoritative interpretations of it. Only in this way can any new interpretations be faithful to this exhortation to unity in faith:

I, therefore, a prisoner for the Lord, beg you to lead a life worthy of the calling to which you have been called, with all lowliness and meekness, with patience, forbearing one another in love, eager to maintain the unity of the Spirit in the bond of peace. There is one body and one Spirit, just as you were called to the one hope that belongs to your call, one Lord, one faith, one baptism, one God and Father of us all, who is above all and through all and in all.[54]

NOTES

1. *Documents of Vatican II*, p. 125.
2. *Ibid.*, p. 119.
3. *Ibid.*, p. 120.
4. The dialogues in which Bultmann first proposed his theory are available in English translation: Rudolf Bultmann, *et al.*, *Kerygma and Myth*, edited by Hans Werner Bartsch, translated by Reginald H. Fuller (New York: Harper Torch Books, 1961).
5. *Ibid.*, p. 11.
6. *Ibid.*, p. 19.

7. *Ibid.*, p. 35.
8. *Ibid.*, p. 42.
9. *Ibid.*, p. 211.
10. *Ibid.*, pp. 39–40.
11. 1 Cor. 15:1–11.
12. 1 Cor. 15:17–20.
13. 1 Thess. 4:13–14.
14. 1 Cor. 15:15.
15. 2 Cor. 5:14–15.
16. Gal. 2:20.
17. Phil. 3:7–11.
18. Phil. 1:21–23.
19. Nicene Creed.
20. 1 Cor. 1:17.
21. 1 Cor. 15:1.
22. 1 Cor. 15:11.
23. 1 Cor. 15:3–8.
24. Rom. 1:1–6.
25. Acts 2:36.
26. 1 Peter 1:23–25.
27. Isaiah 40:9–11.
28. Mk. 1:15.
29. Rom. 1:1–2.
30. Exod. 20:1.
31. Deut. 26:5–10.
32. Gerhard von Rad, "The Problem of the Hexateuch," in *The Problem of the Hexateuch and Other Essays*, translated by E. W. Trueman Dicken (London: Oliver and Boyd, 1966).
33. G. E. Mendenhall was the first to call the attention of Biblical scholars to the parallels between Hittite treaty texts and the covenants of Israel with its God. See his "Law and Covenant in Israel and the Ancient Near East," in *The Biblical Archeolgist*, XVII, no. 2 (May, 1954), pp. 26–46, and no. 3 (September, 1954), pp. 49–76. For a useful survey of more recent discussion on the subject, see D. J. McCarthy, s.j., "Covenant in the OT: The Present State of Inquiry," in *The Catholic Biblical Quarterly*, XXVII (1965), pp. 217–240.
34. Deut. 4:7.
35. Gal. 4:4–5.
36. Gal. 1:11–17.
37. 1 Cor. 9:1.
38. Rom. 1:5.
39. Matt. 28:18–20.

40. Lk. 24:44–47.
41. See note 19, *supra*.
42. Acts 3:18–21.
43. Psalm 109:1.
44. 1 Cor. 15:20–28.
45. Rom. 10:13–15.
46. 1 Cor. 12:27–28.
47. 1 Cor. 2:12–13.
48. 1 Peter 1:10–12.
49. Gal. 2:1–2.
50. Gal. 2:6–10.
51. *Documents of Vatican II*, p. 116.
52. Lk. 1:1–4.
53. Acts 20:25–32.
54. Eph. 4:1–6.

3

Reformation and Aggiornamento

James Kelsey McConica, c.s.b.

In the first paper in this volume, it was pointed out that the Christian faith is at root a revelation, and that revelation is intimately connected with the Church. From one point of view, indeed, it may be maintained that the Church is the direct result of the insertion of revelation into human experience. It conserves, in Scripture and Tradition, what was given to the apostles, as Father Robinson pointed out. It may be added that the Church not only *has* traditions—scriptural, dogmatic and ecclesial—but that it *is* essentially *traditio*, the "passing on" of the message and the activity of Christ.

For this reason we are coming at the present time increasingly to the study of the history of the Church, that unbroken thread through time where the work

of God is interlaced with the work of man. The
history of the Church is itself revealing, and it is only
through knowledge of the actual events of church
history that we obtain access to the tradition of the
Church, and acquire the capacity to judge and act con-
formably to the spirit of the Church—acquire, in fact,
that much-discussed capacity, *sentire cum ecclesia.*

My purpose is to consider the most profound crisis
in the recent experience of the Church—before, that is,
the present moment of reappraisal and anxiety. Much
of what we find in this sixteenth-century crisis has, I
believe, a direct bearing on the issues which face us at
present. More, I hope that in doing this we will also
learn something of the way in which the Church responds to revolutionary situations, of the way in which
its unique resources of vitality function to adapt, conserve, and grow. I intend therefore to devote more
than half my study to a considered analysis of the
Reformation crisis, and then to reflect on the implications of this for the present.

I

Many avoid theology these days from fear of wavering
in their Catholic faith, since they see there is nothing that
is not called into question.—Erasmus, *Confabulatio pia,*
1522.

It is generally conceded by contemporary historians
of the Reformation that the issue of corruption in the
Church must be reappraised. By treating it for so long
as a "cause" of the Reformation, we have found the
need to examine it more precisely for what it tells us
of the deeper failures in the relations between the institutional Church and European society. It is evident
that the Church of fifteenth-century Europe had lost
both its capacity to contain the spiritual aspirations of

the people it was professing to serve, and its ability
to change itself internally to meet this crisis. Put
another way, corruption was not new in the fifteenth
century. It is endemic in the life of the Church; indeed,
it began at the Last Supper. What is interesting is
its running contest with reform. Up to the thirteenth
century, the Church always rallied successfully from
its periods of decadence and managed to contain and
use the new spiritual forces which would be unleashed
in these times of tension and protest. From the fourteenth century on, we are aware that this process is
coming to a halt. There is a kind of stasis in the circulation of vital forces. New movements, instead of
being domesticated, are driven out and persecuted.
The last great adaptation was that represented by the
foundation of the mendicant orders, and the appearance of the Inquisition under Dominican auspices was
a malign symptom that the mendicants' successful
adoption of the most valid ideals of the heretical movements they displaced—a life of radical poverty and of
evangelical preaching—came too late for many who
were alienated from the common life of Christendom.

By the fifteenth century we see massive evidence
that this alienation is becoming very widespread indeed. Within the Church we find a devotional life
which was lost in peripheral matters and perverted by
dark obsessions. Outside the Church we have the re-
currence of heretical movements—the Beguines, the
Fraticelli, the Franciscan Spirituals, the various apoc-
alyptic movements—all of which find a common
theme, interestingly enough, in their concern with
poverty. Why poverty? Hans Baron long ago indicated the significance of this concern to the humanists,
its adoption from Franciscan sources, and its symptomatic importance to men attempting to reconcile the

Stoic ideal of a life of private contemplation with the demands of civic activism.[1] I suggest, however, that there are additional elements, away from the concerns of humanist circles. The conscious cult of poverty is in any age perhaps the most conspicuous repudiation of the preoccupations of a corrupt society; it is the banner of alienation from a fallen order. And it is also, traditionally, the ground for the rediscovery of a new sense of community.

Apart from these symptoms of a deep spiritual disquiet there was the complementary evidence that the structure of authority in the Church itself—so imposing in theory—was in practice dismayingly ineffective. In 1454, Aeneas Sylvius, the aging, cultivated humanist, wrote to a friend, "Christendom has no head whom all will obey—neither the pope nor the emperor receives his due. For there is no reverence and no obedience."[2] In four more years he himself would be pope. In ten more years he would be dead, with the problems that he half-understood, unsolved, and his single greatest project, an unregarded crusade, wholly forgotten. He is a symptomatic figure. No pope of the time was more honest, none understood better the new intellectual forces at work in Europe. Above all, his own career illustrates the dilemma of the pre-Reformation Church: wealthy, powerful, a patron of capital and of learning, it was nevertheless unable to respond to the challenge to which these very assets pointed with anything but outdated gestures—the institutional and disciplinary equivalents of crusades—gestures which did nothing to disguise (and indeed made only more evident) the Church's failing prestige and authority. Excommunications and interdicts multiplied, by their very frequency discrediting the sacramental system they were supposed to uphold. The res publica Chris-

tiana was disintegrating beneath the rivalries of the new monarchies, the pressures from the East, and the new competition to partition the world opening to the West. Gone was the common faith in a Christian boundary under universal canon law and the automatic jurisdictional power of the papacy. In the East the papacy had already admitted, by its own arrangements with the Turks, that political dominion might be justified regardless of belief; in the West, Spain and Portugal were learning to make their own decisions with only a formal acknowledgement of papal pretensions over princes. Thus Aeneas Sylvius, who as Pius II would die in the summer heat of Ancona awaiting Venetian galleys which never came to lead a crusade which never sailed, mused: "We look on Pope and Emperor as figureheads and empty titles. Every city state has its king and there are as many princes as there are households." [3]

So the fifteenth century was for European Christendom—as our present century is for us—a time of profound anxiety, and for rather similar reasons. It was not simply the anxiety of an impending disaster—a visitation of plague or of Norsemen. It was something far more profound: an uneasy awareness, amidst much evidence of increasing prosperity and material success, of a fundamental shift in the forces which had created Christendom, of deep, seismic pressures in the cultural landscape which were already threatening to engulf old landmarks with thrusts that defied all efforts at containment. Some of the evidence for this lies closely gathered upon the pages of Huizinga's *Waning of the Middle Ages*. There is more to be found in the efforts of a few contemporaries of genius to understand it. In More's *Utopia*, Machiavelli's *Prince*, and Erasmus's *Praise of Folly*, we find three outstanding examples of

such an attempt, all sharing—amid radical differences
—one outstanding common feature: an awareness that
the present situation of Europe had to be quite freshly
described against the contrasting background of the
old order—the "true" order—which for so long had
stood unchallenged as an accurate account of the state
of things.

This awareness of a glaring contrast between the
alleged true order and the actual state of European
Christendom is one measure of the Church's failure to
respond to the new social and spiritual forces. These
were forces which were generated, by and large, by
the growing class of educated laymen in the cities.
This is too well known to require extended discussion
here, but it is also too relevant to our theme to be
entirely passed over. It is plain that the core of the
discontent, and with that the most important leadership for change, came from this group and from its
adherents. It began, of course, where urban life first
ripened independent of any association with the predominant feudal culture of the North—in Italy. From
the eleventh century, Italy had been the centre of exchange between the Eastern Mediterranean and Western and Northern Europe. In Italy, and those parts of
Europe touched by Italian enterprise, capitalism was
well established by 1300, and with urban capitalism
came the first literate economy in Europe. Bills of sale,
contracts, letters, journals, ledgers—these were the
undramatic heralds of a new society in which the most
revolutionary instrument in the hands of men would
be the printing press. Francesco Datini, merchant of
Prato, left at his death some 500 ledgers, over 150,000
letters, hundreds of deeds, insurance policies, bills of
exchange, and great, beautifully bound *libri grandi*—
double-entry ledgers for each of his houses in partner-

ship, each headed with a motto which announces a
spirit which historians have wanted to call "Protestant"
but which in fact emerged in the heartland of Catholic
Europe: "In the name of God and of profit." [4]

Here was the interior frontier of the European
spirit, not in the North, languishing under a decadent
and nostalgic feudalism, but in the southern city-states,
which provided a natural environment for the rebirth
of classical ideals. Until 1300 Italian culture had been
out of touch with the dominant feudal and ecclesiastical culture centered in the French court. Suddenly,
about 1300, Italy erupted, and the generation of Dante
and Giotto began a cultural hegemony which lasted
for two centuries.

It was to be the turn now of the educated, urban
layman, aristocratic in outlook to be sure, but neither
feudal nor chivalric. The Italian universities were
dominated not by the study of theology, but by the
professions—law and medicine—and by natural philosophy, Averroism. And there was increasing devotion outside the universities to classical culture, where
these citizens of urban republics found models and
kindred spirits in the past. All of this sprang from lay
education in the city communes. In the early fourteenth century, it is estimated, eight- to ten-thousand
boys and girls were learning to read in Florence.[5]
And the communes provided the job opportunities
for which their education prepared them: they were
run by administrators, bureaucrats, and jurists who
were laymen. The result was not merely a new pro-
fessional ideal; as all know who read their works, they
had truly a spirit new to Europe. There was intense
awareness of personality and events, a tendency to
analytical introspection, and at all times a great sensitivity to the world around. In the established religious

life of Europe they found little that was pertinent to
the society they were creating.

Were they anti-religious? Not necessarily. The new
culture was wealthy, aristocratic, urban, and secular,
to be sure, but it was a complement to Christianity,
not a rival to it—at least, not yet. It was a lay morality
alongside that of the clergy and monks and knights,
full of promise as a secular ideal of virtue and the
good life. With all of this went something else that
was new, a sense of the past. They strove for the
ability to place themselves in time with respect to previous ages; they were aware of historic distance. It
was precisely this which gave them the sense that they
were starting something new.

If they did not challenge Christianity as such, they
did offer a challenge to the mediaeval corporate ideal,
in which men and institutions were seen in the light
of their functions—functions which contributed to
the total welfare of a universal Christian society in
organic harmony. This was the ideal; the actuality
was different, and the difference was especially obvious in Italy. The Italian city-states were ambitious,
self-centered, and individualistic, and so, by and large,
were their citizens. From Renaissance Italy, therefore,
emerged the new ideal of freedom for personal development.

Like the mediaeval ideal, which consciously drew
upon the Pauline notion of the organic unity of the
Christian community, the Renaissance ideology also
had its religious aspect. It recalled the old Christian
theme of the dignity of human nature and the greatness of every individual soul. But life for these Christians was no longer simply a struggle and a pilgrimage;
rather, it was a fine art—the art of harmonious development of body and mind in all their activities. It was,

as we have said, a markedly aristocratic ideal, but it was the ideal of an élite open to creative and intellectual ability. Brains before birth: that was their social creed. Of course it was best to have both.

Now the propagators of this new cultural doctrine, the feverish bearers of the virus, were the humanists. Apart from being the sponsors of a literary science which could have devastating implications for some long-sustained myths, the humanists were élitists with an ideal of state service which appealed to the lay intelligentsia; by and large, they were often Platonists as well. Their Platonism in the first place represented a reaction against Aristotelianism; it was also new and literary, poetic and spiritual. The Florentine Academy founded by Cosimo de' Medici in 1462 with Ficino as life-endowed resident scholar was in many ways the first "free university," making philosophy available outside the Schools. They were also, of course, the pioneer students of the Biblical languages, an outgrowth of the humanists' impassioned concern to revive the true culture of antiquity. This enterprise was sustained and indeed to a large extent made possible by the appearance of the printing press, without which the international humanist community simply could not have worked.

It is clear that there was much in all of this which would embarrass mediocre traditionalists; it also seems clear that it contained the germ of a great Christian revival. Before we turn to their programme for that revival, we should perhaps pause to consider if there was anything in humanism that was essentially subversive of Christianity. We will discount their satire of abuses in the Church and the critical work of Lorenzo Valla on spurious ecclesiastical monuments such as the Donation of Constantine; but as C. S. Lewis

has said, there were trends which contained the
possibility of an open rupture with Christian orthodoxy. In the first place, there is a marked inclination
to mute the Incarnational aspect of Christianity, especially where Platonism enters the humanist stream.
The Incarnation of course they acknowledged, but
the thing that made them breathe more quickly was
the thought of God's immanence. A favourite text
came from the great Johannine prologue: "the light
that lights every man that comes into the world." Interpreted in neo-Platonic terms as metaphysical light,
it became a Form which must be united with all matter if it is to be capable of visibility. God and Christ,
then, permeate all reality. It was of course, up to a
point, part of the central tradition; but it was essentially at variance with the main current from Judaism
through to Aquinas, in which God's immanence was
balanced with His transcendence—His action from a
point utterly outside man's world. In a certain light
it led to a remarkably Sartrian emphasis on man as
self-created, as in the classic utterance by Pico della
Mirandola on "The Dignity of Man." [6]

They were fond, too, of blending all religions and
tolerating all cults, looking for confirmation of Christian doctrine in other religions and purging Christianity itself of elements peculiar to it. Michael Servetus,
the Spaniard concerned for the conversion of Moslems
and Jews, when he discovered that Scripture did not
contain the word "Trinity" or the traditional formula
of substance and persons, jettisoned the whole doctrine for the sake of unity. He was burnt for his pains,
in 1553, in Calvin's Geneva.

Simplification of Christianity—carried on in reaction against a sterile, non-Biblical theology—often had
similar results. The non-dogmatic piety of the Breth-

ren of the Common Life exemplifies this trend, as does that of their pupil, Erasmus, who characteristically followed Gerson and invoked the penitent thief as his patron, since he was saved with so little theology. Implicit in this often very salutary corrective to the nominalistic theology of the Schools was a marked tendency to reduce Christian doctrine to a kind of ethical creed, a blend of Stoicism and the Sermon on the Mount. This trend was most serious when it was combined with a separation of Christianity from its historical core through the allegorical imposition of universal religious meanings. Boccaccio's story of the three identical rings bequeathed by a father to three sons, each of whom believed his own to be unique, is the classic illustration. At the father's death the three proved to be indistinguishable; they were, of course, Christianity, Judaism, and Islam. The story found its great modern exposition, suitably enough, in the age of romantic religious sentimentality and humanitarianism, in Lessing's *Nathan der Weise*.

Humanism was not, then, an attack on orthodox Christianity. To the extent that it was subversive, it was subversive mainly by a subtle transmutation of values, through syncretism, allegorization, moralizing, the reduction of dogma, and the spiritualizing of externals. C. S. Lewis, in a wholly characteristic passage, comments:

In their readiness to accept from whatever source all that seemed to them elevated, or spiritual, or even exciting, we sometimes seem to catch the first faint suggestion of what came, centuries later, to be called, "higher thought." [7]

If we agree, then, that the Church was seriously out of touch with the true spiritual demands of the society developing in fourteenth- and fifteenth-century Europe and that this developing society took its character largely from a newly literate urban laity, we should add that their discontents provide the best clue to their unsatisfied aspirations. Without attempting to substantiate this in detail, I think we find that there were two predominant areas of concern. The first of these is the demand for a greater interiority of religion. The multiplication of extra-liturgical devotions, the demand for prayer manuals, Scripture, and works of interior piety all point to this. This demand represented, of course, an overwhelming reaction to the heavily legalistic practises presented to them in the name of official Christianity. Indeed, most of the leading characteristics of Protestantism were already evident in the fifteenth-century Church: decentralization, the preoccupation with personal salvation associated with devotion to the sufferings of Christ, and the neglect of the sacramental order as such, especially the Eucharist. At the same time there was a diminishing concern with the Church as institution, and with dogma, in favour of this personal devotion. It all came to a focus upon one momentous issue—the intense anxiety over justification: how is man reconciled with God? Frustrated by the elusive satisfactions of good works, more and more people took refuge in mysticism, interior devotion, and non-sacramental piety.

Secondly, we detect along with this subjective, individualistic strain a demand for a new understanding of Christian devotion in terms of life on this earth—the great desire, expressed also in the growth of civic humanism, for activity on behalf of family and community. The failure of Pius II's crusade was marvellously symbolic, since the crusades had been the great achievement of—and evidence for—the earlier success of the Church in capturing the imagination of men in a common ideal.

The fundamental question, then, is that of the Church's failure to respond. It was not that consciences were asleep, or that ability was lacking. There were local responses of many varieties. There was the personal rigourism of Savonarola; there was the mysticism of Gerson, St. Bridget of Sweden, Catherine of Siena, Dame Julian of Norwich, and the whole roster of late mediaeval saints. There was the practical pietism of the *Devotio moderna*, Biblical and strongly lay-oriented. There was, of course, the tradition of conciliarism, which at least in its early phases was closely allied with the desire to reform the Church in head and members. Each of these gained some harvest: the Dominican revival around Catherine of Siena, the Windesheim movement which spread from the Brethren of the Common Life throughout the Benedictine communities of Northern Europe. But each, too, was terribly limited in scope, in face of the great task to be done—the need to stir the entire Church to a fresh assertion of the values of the kingdom of Christ; the need for a sense that a fresh start was truly possible. So the critical problem of the Reformation, I believe, is a problem which I will label "immobilism."

There was no mystery about what was wrong with the spirit of the Church, and no pressing need for new legislation. Much would have been achieved if existing legislation could only have been made to work. If that could have been accomplished, it is conceivable that a greater integrity of life would have led to a further measure of needed change, a totally new orientation of spirituality and evangelism, to embrace the emerging world of urban enterprise. It is a striking feature of almost all late-mediaeval reform proposals that they think only in terms of a restoration of the old standards of true practise. Even Nicholas of Cusa, with the most original mind of the age, thought in terms of the restoration of the "image"—a Platonic approach which of course harmonised with Pauline and Patristic doctrine.[8] In lesser men we meet a totally clerical outlook: let there be no simony or pluralism; keep the monks in their cloisters and enforce true poverty; let the bishops everywhere see that the canons are enforced. There were two fatal shortcomings to such approaches: they were unenforcible, as we have seen; they did not meet the temper of the times, by recognizing the aspirations of the new laity.

Why did not the Church respond? Why was it incapable of gathering together the innumerable streams of reform sentiment into a current which could sweep away the encrustations which imprisoned her? This very large problem might be discussed at a number of levels; perhaps the Great Schism was the most glaring evidence of inherent weakness in the governing apparatus of the Church itself, even apart from the tensions and ruptures inflicted by its entanglements with secular authority. But the general answer lies, I think, in an understanding of the liabilities which the Church carried from her historical involvement with the growth of feudal monarchy, and by that I mean not only her involvement with kings and bureaucracies, but with the whole system of tenure of land and offices. The answer lies, in a word, in a concept with which we began—the disunity of Christendom.

Gregory VII and his successors had astonishing success in centralizing the Church in the Roman Curia; they rescued it from partition between ambitious lords and princes. But the mediaeval Church was not even remotely a monolithic unity. The writ of Rome ran everywhere in matters of doctrine—true; but in any other matter, financial, administrative or disciplinary, it had to penetrate a host of barriers. The same was true, *mutatis mutandis*, for archbishops and even bishops. By the fifteenth century, in fact, the whole ecclesiastical system was a pattern of ineffective authority, riddled with privileged enclaves. To pursue this properly would make an already lengthy theme impossibly long, but perhaps we can be excused with one example. The Kingdom of France, with ninety-three bishoprics and fourteen archbishoprics, had no metropolitan see. The primacy was contested among Lyons, the oldest see of Gaul, Rheims, whose archbishop was traditionally a *legatus natus*, and Paris, representing the power of the crown. Within the dioceses themselves, in France as elsewhere, the bishop's authority was frequently more theoretical than real. Many benefices formally in his gift were in fact disposed of by other interests. On the average, a French bishop controlled the patronage of not over half the benefices in his diocese. The rest were disposed of by such jealous and frequently influential entities as monasteries, cathedral chapters, and noble laymen. Beyond this, the number of exempt religious communities grew constantly; at the level of parish life, the mendicant friars were the most conspicuous and troublesome example. Add to these harassments the depredations of royal authority and the papal *plenitudo potestatis*, which together often disposed over the bishop's head of what few important livings he had left in his hands, and the picture of episcopal helplessness is complete.[9]

So general a portrait needs, of course, much shading and qualification, but the point is clear; this was a far more important matter than corruption itself. Alongside it, of course, was the all-pervading legalism of the feudal Church, expressing itself both in moral doctrine and in its tuition in spirituality, and in the miasma of fiscality, a potent inducement to inertia throughout the offices of the clerical ruling order. On the whole there was no mystery about what was wrong with the spirit of the Church. The great need was to mobilize the forces of reform.

The most ominous consequence of immobilism was that it threw the initiative for Church reform into the hands of secular authority. By the late fifteenth century it was clear to any reformer of perception that the only hope for effective action lay in cooperation with the local prince. Thus there appeared one reforming device to meet with significant success: the political prelate, a figure so armed with delegated papal power and so supported by royal authority that nothing could stand in his way. To the mutual benefit of crown and Church he would cut through entrenched interests to dissolve decayed monasteries, reorder ecclesiastical jurisdiction, bring the influence and administration of the Church into some sort of harmony with the growing apparatus of secular government, and, in general, modernize, reform, prune, and retrench. Such was Nicholas of Cusa, who for a time at least carried all before him in a great part of Germany, Austria, and the Netherlands, instituting the decrees of the Council of Basle. Such was the greatest of them all, Cardinal Ximenes, the man who made Spain the leading haven of Erasmian reform principles. Such would Wolsey have been, if he had had the stature of Ximenes, Cusa, or even of the Cardinal d'Amboise in France. But in general, outside of Spain, northern Italy, southern Germany, and to some extent France, little had been achieved of permanent value before the storm broke.

Why did it break? It is a commonplace to say that Luther's revolt made impossible the gradual emergence of reform principles in the Church and instead produced a reaction which completely altered the direction this reform would take. Was it Luther? Many of his ideas had been put forward more than a century before, by Wycliffe, to generate no more than local enthusiasm in England and Bohemia. Luther was a greater man in personal genius, in radicalism, boldness and energy, and he confronted a Christian society even further advanced in disillusion and decay. There is evidence, however, that this decay was just beginning to recede before the spreading conviction that things must be set right. What turned the crisis of reform into revolution was the interplay of a host of other factors which may be indicated conveniently (if, inevitably, inaccurately) in the symbolic coincidence of two events, one in the world of ideas, the other in the world of politics, and both associated with a famous name. The names are those of Charles V and Erasmus.

In the course of every revolution there is a moment when a vital inner cord snaps, a moment of which you can say that, after that time, there was no turning back. In political revolutions this moment is often fairly easy to locate: the convening of the Estates General or the calling together of the First Continental Congress. Is there any equivalent in the history of the Reformation? Not, I think, in the same sense; the Fifth Lateran Council proclaimed once more the old, futile standards of true observance, and was almost universally ignored by those most concerned with reform.

But there is one political event the momentous consequences of which were foreseeable even at the time.
When Charles of Burgundy, heir to the greatest ap-
panage of political authority the world had seen since
the Caesars, was elected Holy Roman Emperor, it was
predictable that France and the German princes would
seize the first opportunity which offered itself to de-
molish as much of this awesome accumulation as they
could manage to touch. And that opportunity was
presented at the same hour by a brilliant and tor-
mented monk with a mission to purify the Church.

Even more profound, however, was the movement
associated with the name of Erasmus. He was not, of
course, the originator of the movement which takes
his name. Christian humanism had already emerged
by 1510 as the most promising of the movements of
reform—as the only one which grasped the need to
extend the traditional boundaries of Christian enterprise. Why then, are we justified in using the name of
Erasmus to describe it? Because after Erasmus there
is a tremendous difference. The movement of Christian humanism sweeps across national boundaries and
takes on an irresistible evangelical impetus. This was
already evident in men like Wimpfeling, Colet, Le-
fevre d'Etaples, and Contarini, but it was Erasmus who
gave the movement its public character. He was its
prophet and most prolific propagandist, and—preeminently—its scholar-hero. He fused the various com-
ponents of reform into a positive creed and programme
for a new Christian culture, a culture which would
entirely embrace the values and aspirations of the
classically nourished, urban middle classes, and direct
them to Christian ends. Into this creed entered the
pietism of the *Devotio moderna*, the new scripture-
scholarship of Valla, the neo-Platonism of Florence,

and the laicism of those who thirsted for a theology the layman could understand, which would provide the key to a recognized lay vocation within the Christian Church. What is more, Erasmus contributed more than any other humanist to the discrediting of the *status quo* by his probing and restless gift of satire. Finally, he had access everywhere to the centres of power and influential opinion: he alone had a truly European constituency. He formed the conscience of a whole generation, a generation of men and women determined that they had had enough of things as they were. He did what no movement or institution had been able to do before him—he forged the various local and individual impulses to reform into an international crusade under a common creed, and through his monumental endeavours to restore the scriptures and the Fathers he provided his adherents with a sense that a fresh start was, indeed, possible. This programme did embrace the new temper of the times, seeing the need for fresh enterprises rather than the reassertion of old disciplinary ideals, and in that sense it was truly *évangélisme*, the title by which—but for modern associations—it might more properly be known. The creed of Erasmus and his co-workers was the *philosophia Christi*—the Christian culture of the educated layman, steeped in the message of the Gospels and liberated from those speculations of the Schools which were the exclusive monopoly of clerical initiates, and which polluted the pure strain of Christian tradition with the profane categories of Aristotelian rationalism. The phrase *philosophia Christi* itself describes the ideal—a life infused in thought, sentiment and behaviour with the Gospel of Christ, a life of conversion and interior commitment.[10] The "inner religion" is constantly urged as the true way to salvation, opposed to "Judaism"—the confusion of fidelity to Christ with fidelity to external observances. The emphasis is not upon mystical union, but on practical, daily piety, nourished by the reading of Scripture and prayer. In that satirical attack which was the cutting edge of the *philosophia Christi*, the target was legalism and merely formal religious observance. It is hard to deny that this was the characteristic failing of daily religion in Erasmus's day. The multiplication of devotions and pilgrimages, the founding of chantries, of vicariates and prebends, the payments for special prayers, the indulgences—all witnessed to a state of affairs in which salvation, by and large, had become an administrative jurisdiction of the Church.

The genius of Erasmus was to see through the mass of abuses and corruptions to this fundamental problem; to see that no amount of discipline which merely restored true "observance"—the byword of all officially sponsored reform proposals—could restore the integrity and hence the authority of Christian worship without an additional dismantling of this tottering feudal, legalistic superstructure, with its firm clerical underpinnings, in favour of the humanistic culture of the bourgeois layman. Finally, the content of the faith itself was to be carefully scrutinized until the essential elements were discerned, elements which were found in the Gospels and the early Creeds, so that the pure light of evangelical doctrine would leap forth undimmed from the tangle of definitions, opinions and speculative refinements which was the melancholy legacy of theological Aristotelianism and an over-active *magisterium*. In the traditional scholastic sense, the *philosophia Christi* was untheological. It rejected the notion of theology as a science (as did Luther) in favour of the more patristic view that it should be an eloquent persuasion to piety and virtue. Its purpose was not to speculate; it was to improve the lives of men. Unquestionably its strength lay in its elevation of the layman's vocation, which was seen as the potential source of new life in a Church and society fallen into decay.

The new Gospel at once found its enemies. Indeed, it sought them out. We have referred already to its cutting edge, the brilliant satire of the *Colloquies*, and, preeminently, of the paradoxical *Praise of Folly*. Often, Erasmus touched on themes like justification by faith which, once Luther had appeared, sounded like heresy. "Monasticism is not piety." "Christ is the sole head of the Church." "Once Luther had appeared . . .": that is the sad keynote. The theology of Erasmus, undoctrinaire, practical, accommodating, skeptical of the high refinements which had engrossed the mediaeval Schools, had to suffer the fate of all middle positions once the lines of battle had been drawn. It was crushed between advances from both sides. His greatest weakness, in the end, was his presupposition of Catholic orthodoxy as a common ground of debate.

There were other weaknesses, too. The Christian humanists were altogether unsystematic. They overestimated the role of education, and they were far less well-informed than they thought they were about the primitive sources of faith which they recommended so fervently.[11] Like all humanists, they were essentially élitist, fearing popular movements and totally dependent upon the support of princes. More important, once their orthodoxy was questioned, was their Philistine attitude to the established theology. However inadequate or inappropriate they felt it to be, by disdaining any communion with those who espoused it they cut themselves off from the living tradition of theological discourse, and when the crunch came, they were disastrously vulnerable. But none of these weaknesses need perhaps have been fatal if it had not been for the breakdown of the European order in a prolonged conflict over Hapsburg power, and if it had not been for the appearance of radical heresy powerfully sponsored.

Erasmus knew it all. He wrote in 1521:

> . . . to speak frankly, if I had foreseen that an age such as this would arise, either I would not have written certain things which I did write, or I would have written them in a different way. . . . No name is more hateful to me than that of conspiracy or schism or faction.[12]

His final repudiation of Luther was bitter indeed. At first he had been sympathetic, but from the first he pleaded for moderation and open discussion of the issues on both sides. Soon Luther found him pusillanimous; Erasmus found Luther impossible. Worst, Luther's violence endangered the future of his own programme for reform: "If it is right to hate anyone because of personal offenses, the Lutherans have injured no one more than me." On Luther he urged confidence in the clement Leo XI and the "mild and placable" emperor; the decisions of those by whose will human affairs are governed must, he thought, be left to the Lord. "If they prescribe what is right, it is proper to obey; but if what is unjust, it is a holy act to bear it lest anything worse happen." It was all in vain; the Lutherans publicly accused him of cowardice and rushed to their warfare against Rome. In April 1526 Erasmus wrote his final word to Luther. It concluded thus:

> It does not matter what happens to us two, least of all

to myself who must shortly go hence, even if the whole
world were applauding us: it is *this* that distresses me, and
all the best spirits with me, that with that arrogant, im-
pudent, seditious temperament of yours you are shattering
the whole globe in ruinous discord, exposing good men
and lovers of good learning to certain frenzied Pharisees,
arming for revolt the wicked and revolutionary, and in
short, so carrying on the cause of the Gospel as to throw
all things sacred and profane into chaos; as if you were
eager to prevent this storm from turning at last to a
happy issue. I have ever striven towards such an opportunity. What you owe me, and in what coin you have re-
paid me—I do not go into that. All that is a private matter;
it is the public disaster which distresses me, and the irre-
mediable confusion of everything, for which we have to
thank only your uncontrolled nature, that will not be
guided by the wise counsel of friends, but easily turns to
any excess at the prompting of certain inconstant swin-
dlers. I know not whom you have saved from the power
of darkness; but you should have drawn the sword of
your pen against those ungrateful wretches and not against
a temperate disputation. I would have wished you a better
mind, were you not so delighted with your own. Wish
me what you will, only not your mind, unless God has
changed it for you.[13]

In the diary of Albrecht Dürer there is a touching entry at the moment when he heard, in 1521, that Luther
had been imprisoned:

I do not know whether he is still alive or was murdered.
. . . O all ye pious Christians, join with me in heartfelt
mourning for this man, inspired by God. Pray God that
another may be sent in his place, as enlightened as he.
O Erasmus of Rotterdam . . . see how the filthy tyranny
of worldly might and the powers of darkness prevail!
Hearken, knight of Christ, ride at the Lord's side, defend
the truth and grasp the martyr's crown! [14]

Poor Dürer had the wrong man. Even if Erasmus had
identified his cause with that of Luther, he did not
aspire to the crown of martyrdom. Dürer's knight of
Christ was the same who, when asked what he would
do if the Lutherans offered him the choice of accept-
ing their creed or death, replied, "I would imitate St.
Peter, and renounce my faith."

II

The failure of Erasmus, it has been said, was Europe's
tragedy. Certainly in the history of the Church, it is
the crucial link between his time and our own. With
the élite of Europe captive to his pen, the forces of
spiritual regeneration united in a common programme,
and the progress of learning accelerating with every
year, why did Erasmus fail? He failed before the ex-
tinction of European peace, and the appearance of
militant heresy. The latter frightened the leaders of
the Church away from their discipleship to Erasmus,
the former guaranteed powerful political support for
any movement which could be deflected against the
first great threat to the balance of power among the
new nation states. While the Lutheran movement
grew, nurtured by the fervour of men freed from the
tyranny of spiritual legalism and protected by German
princelings terrified at the spectacle of a Hapsburg
powerful enough to realize at last the dream of a
united Germany, the enemies of Erasmus strove to
identify his cause with Luther's own: *Erasmus posuit
ova, Lutherus eduxit pullos*—but "God grant that we
may smash the eggs and stifle the chicks." The mis-
leading view that Erasmus fathered Lutheranism
started with his mendicant enemies and was eventually
perpetuated by Protestant scholars anxious to claim
his scholarly prestige for the common cause against

Rome. But despite its shortcomings (and they have bedevilled Reformation scholarship for generations) this thesis contains an important truth; the work of humanistic evangelism, by satirizing abuses, questioning the traditional authority of scholastic theology and Roman Curia alike, probing difficult and embarrassing questions and proclaiming everywhere the Gospel message of lay devotion, constituted an important achievement of pre-evangelism. In the ground they had prepared were sown the seeds of a doctrine which many of his disciples found ultimately as repugnant as did Erasmus himself.[15] Yet they were hard-pressed to preserve their own cause against an increasingly militant reaction. After Charles V had been chastened by the sack of Rome and the growth of internal dissension in the Empire, Erasmus lost the support of his most influential protector. In Paris, Louis de Berquin, the French translator of Erasmus, Hutten and Luther, was burned at the stake. Erasmus's own writings were condemned by the theological faculties of the Sorbonne and Louvain. In Spain, the Inquisition, at one time the most effective protector of his disciples, began its melancholy purge. Yet in the last year of his life, Alessandro Farnese, now Pope Paul III, offered him a cardinal's hat, a symbol of the underground persistence of his ideas even in a frightened Church.[16]

His party, under enormous pressure, evacuated its middle position. Some disciples chose Rome—the advocates of an Erasmian Catholicism represented in the highest councils by the reforming cardinals Contarini, Sadoleto, Morone, and Pole. Others, despairing of Roman policy, chose Protestantism—an Erasmian Protestantism: Melanchthon, Bucer, the Spaniard Encinas. In one instance the Erasmian creed found a home in a major established church of the reform, in England. Otherwise its influence was mostly underground or indirect, or exerted outside the fold of Christian congregations in the new vein of skeptical humanism announced by Montaigne.

Certain conclusions now emerge. If our reading of the matter is correct, the central issue was not corruption, but the collision between an immobile, hierarchic ecclesiastical structure and the aspirations of a reform movement which was backed by a newly literate laity. This lay group was intensely conscious of a new providential role in the development of society, a role as yet unrecognized by the established traditions of the Church. It had provided itself with an authentic culture that was strongly secular in tone, although it was capable of drawing, also, on deep Christian roots. It was conscious of new power, economic and political —the new monarchs were after all among the newly literate laymen of the day—and, as events proved, it did in fact have the influence to reshape ecclesiastical structures to suit its purposes. It is not true that there was no promise of reform; indeed, there is every evidence that a new texture of Christian thought was beginning to appear, woven from the threads of mediaeval piety, from a new appreciation of the sources of Christian tradition, and from the various creeds of classical origin which appealed to the urban intelligentsia. Ponderous as was the superstructure of feudal responsibility which the Church had inherited, there is reason to think that in time this ferment could have penetrated even the immobility of the late mediaeval Church and brought about a revitalization of the entire Christian body. What its true promise was, we shall never know. The momentous accident of Luther's appearance in the context of the greatest international crisis between the death of Charlemagne and 1789 provoked armed revolt and a warfare of rival orthodoxies supported at sword point. It was not a happy environment for the dispassionate discovery of dogmatic truth.

Instead, the promise of the pre-reform movement was blighted in the mutual intolerance of unilateral orthodoxies, and an apparently impassable gulf was established especially between the Catholic Church and the reformed churches of the Protestant tradition. The real gains were for the forces of secularism: the new monarchies, whose jealousy of power had contributed so heavily to the problems of the late mediaeval Church, made good their most ambitious dreams of dominance over power ecclesiastical in the Protestant establishments; they did almost as well with Rome, through the concordat system. Moreover, the narrowly conceived traditions of rival orthodoxies were too rigid to accommodate the expansive power of the new intellectual currents, especially those with a technological and scientific bent. The divorce of religious and secular culture, the characteristic note of modern European intellectual life, had begun.

What of Rome itself? Was its reaction to the Reformation simply one of retrenchment and failure to grow? It is another commonplace that the reaction to Protestant doctrine was simply to trumpet more loudly the traditional Catholic view. In fact, this is much less true of the decrees of Trent, which were in fact a conservative compromise, than of the effective interpretation they were often given by later generations. The greatest success, as might be expected in a Church so preponderately clerical, was with ecclesiastical discipline: that the standards of clerical integrity have been maintained with remarkable fortitude ever since is a point which Protestant leaders at the present are very willing to concede. The laity fared less well, since much of the achievement in discipline was attained through tightened clerical control. The demand for a modern education in tune with the needs of the day *was* met, for a time at least, and it was met for a century by the Jesuits with a success which compelled the admiration of the whole of Europe. On the side of spirituality, in place of a lay devotional literature as such, lay piety was assimilated to clerical patterns, and was closely associated with clerical supervision—the age of the sodality, of spiritual direction, and of retreats had been born. The clergy retained their monopoly of technical theology divorced from the new intellectual currents, and the laity were given, on the whole, a non-theological, pietistic devotional system, with an intense emphasis—reflecting late-mediaeval interests—on a personal, introspective and individualistic non-liturgical spirituality.

Nevertheless, there was remarkable evidence of the nascent vitality of the Roman Church, perhaps partly because her theology was inherently much more in tune than were the rival systems with the values of an age which loved the order of creation. If the love of Catholic humanists for the native achievements of the human spirit was to some extent muffled in the new air of stern and puritanical pietism which settled over post-Tridentine Rome, it flourished uninhibited and free in the exuberant artistic propaganda of the baroque age. Moreover, catechesis was developed after Protestant models, clerical negligence was heavily punished, the lines of communication between Rome and the bishops were cleared as much as concordats would allow, and the bishops in turn were allowed more truly to govern their dioceses. The result was a surprising reassertion of Catholic vitality, expressed by a vigorous missionary enterprise all along the new frontiers of European technology, and by the domestic revival of a fervent spirituality, a spirituality at once mystical and practical, the spirituality of which Theresa of Avila is the greatest prototype.

There is no time here to discuss the details of the achievement and limitations of the Catholic reform. Instead, it may be characterized well by a phrase of Yves Congar: its achievement was to overcome the perennial temptation of the Church to Pharisaism—to making the means of salvation ends in themselves.[17] This is not to say that this tendency has not persisted, but that, by and large, the simple fact that the true object of the Church's mission is the elevation of man to share in the divine life has always been much more evident since the Council of Trent. To that extent at least, it responded to the essential critique of the Erasmian reformers. The limitation of the Catholic Reform was its decision to become a synagogue—to become, within the European scene, a self-sufficient, enclosed entity; effectively, a sect. In place of concentration on essentials of the faith, there was concentration on the distinguishing marks of Catholicism; in place of a renewal of theology, there was a growing process of alienation from the evolution of Western thought. Sociologically, the process was marked by a growing identification of the Church with the interests of ruling houses and fading aristocracies on the one hand, and of the peasantry on the other—an ironic process of "feudalizing" after the day of feudalism had passed, and along with it the day of the Church's true social universality. It should be noted that there was one

exception, in time to be of momentous importance—
the remote colonization of a Catholic population in
North America.

As generations passed it became more and more
evident that the temptation to the synagogue was a
costly temptation indeed. Embattled, alien, proud and
suspect, the Church could maintain its isolation only
at the cost of periodic scandal (the Galileo episode remains the classic issue), of iron discipline, and of recurrent purges. Thus Lord Acton, perhaps the most
learned Catholic of his generation, could write in the
Home and Foreign Review of April, 1864, eight
months before the promulgation of *Quanta cura* and
the *Syllabus of Errors*, as follows:

Among the causes which have brought dishonour on
the Church in recent years, none have had a more fatal
operation than those conflicts with science and literature
which have led men to dispute the competence, or the
justice, or the wisdom, of her authorities. . . . They
have induced a suspicion that the Church, in her zeal for
the prevention of error, represses that intellectual freedom
which is essential to the progress of truth; that she allows
an administrative interference with convictions to which
she cannot attach the stigma of falsehood; and that she
claims a right to restrain the growth of knowledge, to
justify an acquiescence in ignorance, to promote error,
and even to alter at her arbitrary will the dogmas that
are proposed to faith.[18]

This costly decision by the post-Reformation Church
to reform by discipline linked to disengagement has
led us once more to a situation in which there is deep
concern that the institutional Church is radically out
of touch with the demands of Christian society. There
is an ironic measure both of the achievement and of
the shortcomings of the Catholic reform in the fact

that, while in the fifteenth century the reformers are
united in demanding a desecularization of a much too
worldly Church, the contemporary cry is for the
Church to be reborn in the secular city.

We find, too, many parallel symptoms between the
crisis of the Reformation and the tensions of today.
There is once more a sense of anxiety from a frag-
menting of the Church's authority: Pope Paul VI
might echo the complaint of Pius II that there is "no
head whom all will obey." There is the same awareness of new social and political forces which threaten
the integrity of Catholic culture. There is once more
a tendency to mute the Incarnational aspect of Christianity in favour of a humanistic Christ, accompanied
by a doctrine of ethical Christianity mounted through
a social gospel. There is syncretism, evident in the
desire to mute the peculiar doctrines of Christianity in
favour of the enlightened conscience of non-believers.
There is a marked Philistinism towards traditional
technical theology combined with a flight into a kind
of para-theology based on philosophical currents alien
to the central tradition of the Church—most of them
now post-Hegelian. Once more there is a marked return *ad fontes*, to Scripture and the Fathers, characteristic of all ages of reform. And once more this is
linked with insistence on bringing this knowledge to
the layman, and on the circulation of informed opinion about Scripture which is accessible to everyone.
Once more there is insistence on vernacular liturgy,
and on worship which reflects the demands of the
iocai community. With all of this there is a realization of the Erasmian dream of a popular circulation of
theological works which would delight the heart of
the retiring and acerbic Dutchman. Once again there
is a strong reaction against a legalistic moral system

of prescriptions, pains and penalties, and against extra-liturgical devotion, in favour of piety centered on the person of Christ and in favour of sanctification through charitable works—the active apostolate.

Is there anything to parallel the anxiety over justification? It is possible that there is, and it is at quite a deep level. It seems evident that there is a current of opinion running against the entire sacramental system in favour of something like justification by faith. It is usually not far removed from the gospel of "love" understood primarily as an answer to human isolation. This is, I suspect, closely tied to another interesting parallel. The justification controversy of the sixteenth century grew, in part, from the "retreat of God" which came about, largely, through nominalistic theology. In an attempt to rescue God's omnipotence and dignity it had in many ways succeeded in making Him utterly remote, capricious and inscrutable. The anxiety over justification in the sixteenth century was a knot formed from this sense of the terrible remoteness of God, from legalistic devotions, and from an equally legalistic moral theology in the confessionals. In the background to the present controversy these latter elements are still often present; the first—the remoteness of God—has been reincarnated as the "death of God"—the feeling that the God of traditional theology is so remote from the concepts and values of contemporary thought as to be entirely meaningless. As a result the present anxiety over justification is not seen so much as a problem of relating man to God, as of relating man to his fellow man. Recently it has become clear that the initial success of the liturgical reform and the theological revival grounded upon the notion of salvation history has not concealed a fundamental debate on the very meaning of salvation. It is possible to predict that we are very soon to hear much more about the Modernist crisis, the Banquo's ghost at many a liberal theological *agapé*.

What do these parallels mean? How do we read the symptoms? It is clear, I think, that the Church is once again undergoing the shock of reappraisal induced by an awareness that her established procedures, structures, and pastoral attitudes contrast sharply with the actual state and outlook of society. One consequence is the renewed search for essentials, closely parallel to the Erasmian quest for the essentials of the faith. To this I will return in a moment. Many of the parallels are the predictable accompaniment of any period of intense doctrinal debate, and many, like the élitist tendencies of coterie theologies, have no profound implication for the life of the Church at large. But some of the parallels we have noticed occur because of an additional factor. One of the major elements in the Reformation crisis looms just as large today—the demands of a laity, profoundly sympathetic with secular values, educated, resentful of the ancient clerical monopoly of theological learning, and united, informed, and occasionally misled by a revolution in communications at least as profound as that of printing. We find among them, too, an ideal of state service and social concern, and we find it markedly in North America where a Catholic middle class not only survived but flourished and prospered under the paternal rule of a disciplined and highly regulative clerical Church. It is not difficult to explain why it is on this continent that the post-Vatican-II atmosphere most closely parallels developments of the early sixteenth century.[19]

If we are struck by parallels, however, we must also note important differences. The first is the freedom of the modern Church from the synthetic feudal alliance of the seventeenth century. The involvement with dynasties and aristocracies was forcibly stripped away by the time of Vatican I. It is no accident that it was immediately after the loss of temporal power that the modern Church showed the first signs of willingness to move forward; significantly, it was in the realm of social policy, under Leo XIII. Today, the political involvement of the Church is so local as scarcely to matter in the struggle over renewal. It does not matter that this freedom has been by and large forced upon the Church rather than sought. For the same reason, the modern movement for reform lacks the highly inflammable material of widespread decadence and corruption. Modern Catholicism continues to err through legalism, but the marks for integrity in general are very good.

And this point is immediately related to the most striking difference of all: the difficulty in attempting to compare the present situation of the Church to its trial of "immobilism" in the sixteenth century. The Second Vatican Council is the realization, four hundred years after the day, of the great dream of the pre-reform party: a council directed not simply toward the reassertion of old standards of observance, but precisely toward an awakening of the conscience of the Church at every level. The importance of this is even clearer if you attempt to find a modern equivalent of Erasmus's *Enchiridion militis Christiani*, the manifesto and handbook of the Christian humanist party. There are many distinguished candidates, but the real discovery of this exercise is that no one work had the impact and widespread significance in moulding the outlook of the reforming generation that Erasmus's writing had. There is only one body of material which has the universal impact of the *Enchiridion*, and that is the collection of council decrees. It is a remarkable fact that, like the *Enchiridion* itself, they too are predominantly hortatory and normative, not doctrinal. In a profound sense they are prophetic, in that they interpret the present condition of the people of God in the light of eternal destiny.

There is, then, no crisis of immobilism in the earlier sense. There is, however, a kind of immobilism difficult to distinguish, at times, from apathy or despair, a reluctance to change when the direction of change is so uncertain. This may produce a resort to the narcotic of nostalgia: Vatican II was a mistake. It may, on the other hand, produce a drift into indifference or hostility: the Gospel is "irrelevant." What many Catholics are waiting for, no doubt, is a fresh Christian vision of our situation which goes beyond the achievement of Vatican II; this, quite clearly, is the attraction exerted by a Teilhard de Chardin.

The new directions eventually found will emerge, no doubt, from a complicated procedure now under way, the fresh quest for essentials. We have seen that this was one of the standards carried by the Erasmian reformers; it is also the unarticulated platform of many contemporary theologians. The highly sensitive issue of the development of doctrine is in fact precisely this question. If it is true that in the sixteenth century the sudden fresh contact with classical culture helped the Christian humanists to discern what was worth preserving from the mediaeval heritage, the problem today is surely that there is no simple single corpus of learning which can act in quite the same way.

There are two procedures under way, however, which are promising to perform this function. The first of these is the recurrent resort of the Church to renewed study of Scripture and the early Fathers.

About this little need be said. But there is another process under way which is closely related to this, although it is more characteristic of the modern mentality, and that is the renewed concern with Church history. Given that the Church of faith and the Church of history are one reality, in the history of the Church we may learn a great deal to distinguish between those elements in her life which are of the essence and those which are of transitory importance.

This is particularly evident when we turn to consider one of the structural changes brought about by Vatican II, a change which is an essential complement to the procedures of self-examination currently under way, and that is the concept of collegiality. Hubert Jedin has recently written that an ecclesiology which is not nourished by church history is like a frame without a picture.[20] In the constitution *De Ecclesia*, the relation of the episcopal college to its head, the pope, is called *communio*. It is impossible to understand the content of this notion without knowing how and in what forms *communio* was experienced in the ancient Church; that, for example, which Irenaeus wanted to indicate by saying that Pope Anicetus and Polycarp "communicated together": it was not only a question of communication in the true faith, but also of the Eucharistic community, of remembrance in the dyptics, and of the incessant correspondence of the individual churches among themselves and with the bishop of Rome. The introduction of episcopal conferences will appear alarming only to those who know nothing about the synodal structure of the ancient Church, and who do not know that the fiscal centralization at the end of the Middle Ages and the liturgical and administrative centralization after the Council of Trent were forms "conditioned and justified by the era, but not the only possible form of the exercise of papal primacy." The powers assigned to the episcopal conferences are not a break with the tradition of the past; they are a restoration of a collaboration which once existed between the popes and the bishops, between the Roman Church and the particular churches for the good òf the Universal Church, and this restoration corresponds to the need of the world-wide Church of the twentieth century. Four centuries ago Melchior Cano, the founder of theological methodology, said: *Viri omnes docti consentiunt rudes omnino theologos illos esse, in quorum lucubrationibus historia muta est.* It is probably true to say that it was necessary to wait for the one world of modern technology before the Roman communion, with its vast, international community, could experience something like collegiality, something which up to this time has been the property only of provincial or more static and confined traditions: the Church of England or the Orthodox Church.

Linked with the sacramentality of the episcopate, the first signification of collegiality, it is worth recalling, is that of unity—unity of faith and sacrament in the life of the Spirit in the Church assembled about its priests and bishops. Yves Congar has written that the doctrine "will appear as balancing and complementary only with time as future events bear out." [21] Historically, it recalls the great concern of the Reformation with the calling of frequent councils and the reassertion of episcopal rights. It points, therefore, to old remedial and regenerative forces—the reassertion of episcopal authority and the emphasis on consultation—but it is directed this time not to purification and discipline, but to the opening-out of the Church to the world. Moreover, the concept of collegiality is much more profound, theologically, than was any doctrine of the conciliar movement. It runs from the ultimate authority in the Church down to the level of parochial organization, and it will take generations for its full implications to be realized. But the direction of that movement seems clear. It is not towards a completely lay Church: that experiment flowered and faded in the wilderness of Geneva. It is toward a more open ecclesiastical polity, one in which the richness of debate and local tradition will ultimately enhance the unity which is the condition of the Church's existence and the source of its vitality—the unity of the body of Christ.

On the level of doctrine the great theme of this present age is, I think, a theme which links us most deeply to the crisis of the sixteenth century. It is the need to incorporate into Christian teaching the humane moral values which emerged in Renaissance Europe, which have been heightened in modern times by a growing sense of man's capacity for control of nature and for self-improvement. In his opening address to Vatican II, Pope John XXIII said of modern men that

They are ever more deeply convinced of the paramount dignity of the human person and of his progress to perfection, as well as of the duties which that implies.[22]

We have now come some way from the sixteenth century and it seems very likely that we do have the theological concepts which will allow us to deal with this problem.[23] They lie in the theme of "graced nature," nature which is already redeemed, the only nature which we actually know. This allows us to hold that by adhering to the norms of nature with reason and integrity, a man can indeed transcend himself, even apart from an explicit belief in God, provided that such lack of belief is not culpable. This is the theme which unites the various enterprises of such different but profoundly influential figures as Teilhard de Chardin, Blondel and Karl Rahner. Their common concern, like that of Erasmus and More and their companions, is to insist that man's spiritual perfectibility is a capacity interior to his nature as redeemed, and not a matter of conformity to standards extrinsic, alien and remote. It is—in its orthodox formulation at least—the great vision of St. Paul, of a whole creation groaning for redemption, a creation in which man has the pre-eminent role, and in which he is entirely at home, playing his part in the *mysterion*—the hidden plan of God for the redemption of the cosmos. With the humanists they reject the late-scholastic view that the perfection of man is extrinsic to his personal moral development, and they reject also the solution of Luther that the perfection of man is due to the grace of God alone without any reference to man's own free will. In the end, the victory has gone to the humanists, insisting that the teachings of the great pagan moralists and the evangelical counsels form a continuum, and that both are part of the economy of grace and salvation. It is this delicate but profound theme which is today being resumed, and upon its development—rather than upon the superficial issues of contraception and clerical celibacy which captivate the popular press—that there rests the future of a valid *aggiornamento* of Christian teaching.

In summary, I would say that the forces released by Vatican II have been deeply disturbing precisely because the council dealt accurately with the true problem of the modern Catholic Church—the failure of the synagogue. That the impulse came from the top is the best evidence that the problem of immobility is radically different from that in the sixteenth century. It will remain to trouble local churches for a long time, but it seems safe to say that the process of ferment and change is guaranteed by the very forces which the new vision of the Church presupposes: the existence of an international community of Catholics, lay and clerical, instructed and informed, and involved in open debate at all levels of the Church. Does this mean that the Church will be defenseless against heterodoxy? Not at all. The long history of an exclusively centralized structure has robbed us of any understanding of the way in which the consensus of the Church can discern and expunge false doctrine. But to see the process in active operation, read the history of the Arian controversy, or study the struggle against Pelagianism.

This is as much as I can say on the basis of parallels with what has gone before; perhaps the real conclusion is that the present experience of the Church is as unprecedented as it is full of promise. In the past, such trials have always been a prelude to the resurgence of unexpectedly vigorous new life. Considering the same precedents, it seems certain that this new life will appear without being recognized at once. As Jean Guitton has recently written of the sixteenth century crisis, "Men are blind to the new beginnings of their own day. The new birth slips in quietly and surely, and takes hold in the substance of things." [24] But in this new birth we have no choice but to take part, in all sobriety of mind. This point also was best put by Lord Acton:

From the beginning of the Church it has been a law of her nature that the truths which eventually proved themselves the legitimate products of her doctrine, have had to make their slow way upwards through a phalanx of hostile habits and traditions, and to be rescued, not only from open enemies, but also from friendly hands that were not worthy to defend them.[25]

It is hard to be patient, and it requires faith and discernment and toughness of mind. What we are now witnessing is the curious internal dialectic by which the Church learns, suffers, and progresses; only this time it is proceeding openly and not in secret and subterranean channels. It seems to me that we must expect provisional solutions while this internal dialectic proceeds. We should not be so stung by the tensions and embarrassments which this causes that we render ourselves unable to appreciate what a striking testimony to the confidence and integrity of the modern Catholic Church this is. If we do not keep the positive elements uppermost in our mind we may find ourselves, in our apathy, the allies of a new and most subtle kind of immobilism, a stagnation of spirit, which recalls the warning question about whether the Son of Man, on His return, would find faith upon the earth.

NOTES

1. Hans Baron, "Franciscan Poverty and Civic Wealth as Factors in the Rise of Humanistic Thought," *Speculum*, XIII, no. 1 (1938), pp. 1–37; cf. G. B. Ladner, "Homo viator: Medieval Ideas on Alienation and Order," *Speculum*, XLII, no. 2 (1967), pp. 233–259.
2. Pope Pius II to Leonardo di Bentivoglio, in J. B. Ross and M. M. McLaughlin, eds., *The Portable Renaissance Reader* (New York: Viking, 1965), p. 75.
3. *Ibid.*
4. W. K. Ferguson, *Europe in Transition, 1300–1520* (Boston: Houghton Mifflin, 1962), pp. 103–104; Iris Origo, *The Merchant of Prato: Francesco di Marco Datini* (New York: Knopf, 1957).
5. Report of Giovanni Villani; see Ferguson, *op. cit.*, p. 278.
6. *The Portable Renaissance Reader*, p. 476.

7. C. S. Lewis, *English Literature in the Sixteenth Century* (Oxford: Clarendon Press, 1954), p. 11, and Introduction.

8. See, e.g., his *De Pace fidei*, edited with a commentary by R. Klibansky and H. Bascour (London: Warburg Institute, 1956).

9. A mass of evidence is scattered throughout the four volumes of G. G. Coulton's *Five Centuries of Religion* (Cambridge: University Press, 1923–50); for a more recent appraisal of the entire system, see W. A. Pantin, *The English Church in the Fourteenth Century* (Cambridge: University Press, 1955).

10. The classical source for the *philosophia Christi* of Erasmus is his *Enchiridion militis Christiani*; an abridged text is conveniently available in *The Essential Erasmus*, translated by John P. Dolan (New York: Mentor-Omega, 1964).

11. Despite the vast editorial efforts of the humanists, a good understanding of even the third century A.D. was not available until about 1530, and the principal works of the second-century apologists were not known until the 1550s. As for the Apostolic Fathers, they were very little known. The Epistles of St. Ignatius appeared in Latin in 1498 but in texts much interpolated; the Epistle of Polycarp of Smyrna to the Philippians appeared in Latin in 1498, but not in Greek until 1633. A bad Latin text of the *Shepherd* of Hermas was published in 1513, but the first Greek text had to wait until 1866. The crucial *Didache*, whose exact dating is still the subject of much dispute, appeared in 1883. Much of the violent battle about the primitive Church in the early sixteenth century was thus fought in serious obscurity. This was a material point for a reform tradition like that of the humanists, whose strongest arguments were founded on the appeal to return to the sources of doctrine and faith.

12. Erasmus to Jodocus Jonas, 10 May 1521; Latin text in P. S. and H. M. Allen, eds., *Opus Epistolarum Des. Erasmi Roterodami*, IV (Oxford: Clarendon Press, 1922), no. 1202; citation from the translation by John C. Olin in *Christian Humanism and the Reformation* (New York: Harper Torchbooks, 1965), p. 160.

13. *Opus Epistolarum*, VI, no. 1688; translation by Barbara Flower in Johan Huizinga, *Erasmus and the Age of Reformation* (New York: Harper Torchbooks, 1957), pp. 241–242.

14. Quoted by Huizinga, *Erasmus*, p. 148.

15. See K. H. Oelrich, *Der späte Erasmus und die Reformation* (Reformationsgeschichtische Studien und Texte, 86 [Münster: Aschendorff, 1961]); also, Andreas Flitner, *Erasmus im Urteil seiner Nachwelt* (Tübingen: Niemeyer, 1952).

16. *Opus Epistolarum*, I, p. 65, XI, pp. 221, 244f. The evidence is not entirely clear.

17. The phrases "temptation of Pharisaism" and "temptation to act like the synagogue" are employed in his *Vraie et fausse réforme dans l'Eglise* (Paris: Editions du Cerf, 1950), Part I, chapter 2, II and III, but with a broader and more systematic purpose.

18. Lord Acton, "Conflicts with Rome," in *Essays on Freedom and Power*, edited by Gertrude Himmelfarb (New York: Meridian, 1955); see Hugh A. MacDougall, *The Acton-Newman Relations* (New York: Fordham University Press, 1962), pp. 88–89.

19. It is interesting to consider the contrast in leadership of opinion between Europe and North America since Vatican II. In Europe the most radical thought comes from clerical voices, while distinguished lay opinion, which held conspicuous authority between the world wars, tends now to show concern for traditional values. In America the most radical voices are those of laymen (including former priests and religious).

20. "La position de l'histoire de l'Eglise dans l'enseignement théologique," *Seminarium*, XIX (January–March, 1967), pp. 130–146. The remarks which follow draw from Jedin's text.

21. *Informations Catholiques Internationales*, 22 (1 December 1964), p. 5; cited by Canon Charles Moeller in *Vatican II: An Interfaith Appraisal*, p. 135.

22. *Council Daybook, Vatican II*, sessions 1 and 2, edited by Floyd Anderson (Washington, D.C.: National Catholic Welfare Conference, 1965), p. 28.

23. See, e.g., A. Levi, s.j., "Renaissance and Reformation," *The Dublin Review*, No. 505 (Autumn, 1965), pp. 255–267.

24. *Great Heresies and Church Councils* (New York: Harper and Row, 1965), p. 145.

25. See note 18, *supra*.

4

Modern Man, Faith, and Doubt

Timothy Suttor

I

IN *The Waste Land*, nearly fifty years ago, T. S. Eliot offered a profound diagnosis of the spiritual condition of twentieth-century Western man by observing how he handles two of the fundamental and inescapable human experiences—sexual union and death. It is above all important for us to follow his approach to the problem of sexuality; to see that while our sexual disorders are real evils in themselves, they in truth speak to us at a level deeper than words of evils far greater—of alienation from God, of intellectual despair, of contempt of life. The Gentiles, wrote Paul to Ephesus, make vain fancies their rule of life because their minds are clouded with darkness. The inflexibility of the secular conscience breeds an ignorance which estranges men from the divine life; and so, in despair, they have given themselves up to incontinence, to selfish habits of impurity.[1] It was in this spirit that Eliot approached the modern city-dweller, and it is in this spirit that we must approach him. We are not to think that the future of belief depends on endless articles with footnotes, when in fact it depends on how urban man comes to terms with being a body in a world of bodies, subject to ignorance, concupiscence, and death. Popular Freudianism imagines that sex-drives lie behind all behaviour. Christianity, on the contrary, has always known that our chaotic sexuality merely dramatizes and acts out our frustration, egotism, and deliberate shutting-off of conscience.

Five lines of *The Waste Land* capture for us the inexpressible yearning, the rapture, the intense feeling for the infinite, which sexual love can engender in the heart:

—Yet when we came back, late, from the Hyacinth
    garden
Your arms full, and your hair wet, I could not
Speak, and my eyes failed, I was neither
Living nor dead, and I knew nothing,
Looking into the heart of light, the silence.[2]

But man's sense of the infinite is starved when doubt and subjectivism are cultural routines, and then superstition comes in to fill the vacuum and the city holds the soul captive; and then it is that sexual love, instead of opening out on God, opens out on death, nothingness, boredom, listlessness. Nothing shows the destructive power of modern doubt more than the moods and forms of modern sexuality. The actual sordidness in which young love's great hopes end is portrayed in the two brilliant scenes of sections II and III of the poem. In lines 100–104 and 203–205 the nightingale, Keats's symbol of beauty, means rape. Lines 139–164 confront us, not merely with adultery and abortion, but also with the destruction of the sense of beauty and *consequently* of the religious and moral sense, and even of love of life:

> . . . think of poor Albert,
> He's been in the army four years, he wants a good time,
> And if you don't give it him, there's others will, I said.
> Oh is there, she said. Something o' that, I said.
> Then I'll know who to thank, she said,
>   and give me a straight look.
> HURRY UP PLEASE ITS TIME
>
>   .   .   .   .
>
> You ought to be ashamed, I said, to look so antique.
> (And her only thirty-one.)
> I can't help it, she said, pulling a long face,
> It's them pills I took, to bring it off, she said.[3]

And so again with the two seductions of section III.

There is no answer in the waste land of modern culture, where Christian faith and martyrdom are a mere memory, the name of a piece of architecture— St. Mary Woolnoth, or Magnus Martyr. Faith's answer comes from beyond, in thunder, as it always comes, and always the same stern old mysterious message. First, complete self-surrender to the exigencies of the spiritual, option for the spiritual *against* the material:

> The awful daring of a moment's surrender
> Which an age of prudence can never retract
> By this, and this only, we have existed [4]

Second, the knowledge that each such surrender is made by each person completely alone with the thought of death, his death, and that the decision for God cannot be evaded when the moment comes, for to fail to decide is itself to make the wrong decision:

> . . . I have heard the key
> Turn in the door once and turn once only
> We think of the key, each in his prison[5]

Third, asceticism, discipline, control; obedience to conscience over fancy, whim, passion, and above all over cultural conformism. And the keynote of asceticism is harmony and lightness of heart, because it is based on complete intellectual certitude touching the unseen, and therefore on the pleasure which floods the personality from this source and from this source only:

> . . . The boat responded
> Gaily, to the hand expert with sail and oar
> The sea was calm, your heart would have responded
> Gaily, when invited, beating obedient
> To controlling hands[6]

Since Eliot's day, progress in the biosciences, more particularly regarding the chemical triggers and timing of ovulation, has much more completely knocked away all the adventitious supports which had shored up the traditional conception that sexual intercourse outside marriage is immoral: I mean that the fear of pregnancy has gone. And it is now not merely possible physically, it is socially quite accepted, for the unmarried as well as the married to have intercourse at any time without conception. This revolution is a *fait accompli* in North America and Europe, particularly among the better-off, and it is stupid to pretend otherwise. The only motive now for chaste continence, or for chaste sexuality, is our need of God. Sexual conduct has become a better symbol than ever of our understanding of God, or rather of our lack of it. In our day, the unchastity which neither desires nor enjoys a serene and convinced mental control of sex-reflexes frequently amounts to an assertion of a philosophical world view at war with Christianity—which is to say, at war with true love. Chastity, the human value on which Vatican II decided to put the emphasis when speaking of marriage, has become an affirmation of a religious view of life and of the world-process. Absolute right and wrong are unintelligible without reference to our need of the absolute God who alone is our happiness; there is no other serious reason for being chaste.

Two basic philosophical positions of our culture wage war on faith under the camouflage of the "sex-revolution": agnosticism, and what, for want of a better term, I shall call pantheistic evolutionism.

By agnosticism I mean the notion that it is impossible to think one's way to clear-cut, objective, irreversible certitude touching the invisible world of spirit. To give a current instance, the request for a papal ruling on the contraceptive pill was agnostic in tendency. For we have papal rulings enough on the subject. What was wanted was really a papal ruling reversing previous papal rulings. There is an insuperable objection to such a course, as there was to any declaration of religious liberty which contradicted the teachings of Leo XIII and Pius XII; if the former contradicted rulings were not irreversible, why should the new one be? Those requesting it either do not notice, or else hope the pope will not notice, that he is being asked to undermine his own teaching authority in the very act of teaching. But where advocacy of the contraceptive pill is innocent, its repudiation could prove providential; it is an ideal way of affirming the reality and primacy of the invisible world, since it shows the power of intellect's passion for truth, for certitude, to govern flesh at its most vehement. Those who make war on the idea of papal infallibility are usually at war with the very concept of absolute religious certitude, an unshakeable grasp of the unseen world that cannot be lost. They are at war, then, with man's strongest, deepest passion; they are at war on themselves. Behind the dogma of papal infallibility, according to the one and only philosophical system the popes themselves recommend, stands the doctrine of the natural infallibility of every human intellect. If the mind of man goes wrong, according to St. Thomas and his school, this cannot be attributed to any defect of its nature. All error traces back to sin.

Christianity is one idea, said Newman, and certitude is of its very essence.[7] It is thus always, of its essence, a philosophy of knowledge, asserting the power of every human mind to reach perfect certitude. But the entire modern era, culturally, is one long crisis centred on the question: can I be *certain* of things beyond the realm of sense? Can I make propositions in religious matters, such as "Christ died for our sins and rose again for our justification," and know that they cannot ever possibly be false? A resolution of this question, this doubt, this conflict, is at the heart of the conversion process in every modern mind. Notice how I phrased the question: can *I* be *certain*? Each man has to answer this question completely on his own, as if no one else had ever faced it. The fact that another man has answered it is of no avail to me when I lie dying. Each man has to see for himself how the denial that certitude is possible, whether in the realm of spirit or in the realm of sense, always is and always has to be a self-refuting position. No matter how great the

philosopher's fame—whether his name be Kant or
John Stuart Mill or Hegel or Husserl or Bergson or
William James or Bertrand Russell—he refutes himself
at an elementary, common-sense level if he denies
man's power to be absolutely and objectively certain,
beyond all fear of error, on matters such as God,
morality, and the after-life. Thus the Kantian position
that we do not know the real but only our categoriza-
tion of it is self-refuting because it is an implied claim
to know the reality called human knowledge. Similarly, the statement that nothing can be asserted unless
it can be verified by sense-observation is itself a statement that cannot be verified by sense-observation.
Dewey has said: "The true is the useful"; nowadays
it is said that the true is the relevant, the contemporary,
the stage reached in history by man's evolving consciousness. But we still want to know, of every such
statement, Is it true? Is that the way things *are*, the
way life *is*?

The discovery of such hidden contradictions is not
an idle game. It was the immediate prelude to the
conversion of Augustine in antiquity. It is a matter of
discovering the intellect's own natural law: that all it
wants is to grasp what really exists, the things that *are*.
No other activity merits the name of thinking. Therefore it is no accident that the Thomistic philosophical
position so consistently recommended by the Roman
Church has, historically, been consistently concerned
to insist on man's ability to know what is what. Nor
is it an accident that when great Christian prophets
arose in the new language-worlds of modern scientific
civilization—for instance, Butler and Newman in England, Kierkegaard in the Germanic area, the Pecci
brothers in Italy, Solovyev in Russia—each rested his
apostolic preaching on a profound defence of the hu-

man mind's power to know the real. The experience
of certitude, and certitude alone, is the key which
opens on to the world of the spirit and its joy without
measure. For here, at the self-critical moment of philosophy, here alone our ego learns that complete surrender to the real which is the condition, naturally,
of surrender to God. Give, and it shall be given to
you: good measure, pressed down, shaken together,
running over. But if you refuse to commit yourself
at this point, faith itself, and hope and love with it,
will be taken away from you.

Augustine wrote over 1500 years ago:

As for the new Academicians, whom Varro avouches to
hold no certainty but this, that all things are uncertain, the
Church of God detests these doubts as madness, having a
most certain knowledge of the things it apprehends. . . .
It believes the evidence of the senses. . . . It believes
also the holy canonical Scriptures . . . from which the
just man has his faith . . . ; this faith being kept firm, we
may lawfully doubt all such other things as are not mani-
fested unto us either by sense, reason, Scripture, or testimony of grounded authority.[8]

Modern doubt is not modern. Faith has aways been
opposed by learned doubt as well as by common
mental laziness. And its central piece of evidence, the
resurrection of Jesus, has always required of men that
they trust their power to know for sure. Trust your
senses and the Apostles' senses; trust the schooling
which hands on the testimony of the Apostles; and
trust your own reasoning powers (for the resurrection
does not directly prove Jesus was God; it proves it
only through indirect reasoning, by arguing that God
would not have raised Jesus from the dead had His
claim to be God been false). Faith's certitude of God's
redeeming love must not be reduced to our trust in the

Apostles' sense-perception, or to our trust in the reliability of the Gospels as records, or to a piece of reasoning based on the event thus known to us. Faith altogether transcends this information. Faith is a lantern in the dark place of our heart, known to us by its own light; faith is God shining on the heart. But faith can live in a mind which accepts the certitudes of experience, history and logic, and faith must die in a mind that denies its own power thus to grasp and explain reality.

The first effect of conversion, or justification, in re-integrating human personality is precisely purity of conscience—which is to say, an unshakeable will not to be deceived, either by denying something to be which is, or by asserting something to be which is not. We rejoice that things are as they are. We do not gamble our happiness on the possibility that we do not exist after death. We confine ourselves to what is certain. And through such purity of conscience, God is indistinctly grasped. From the observed fact of change, implying causality, and our generalization of this into a realization of the contingency of created being, the mind ascends to know God by analogy as the ultimate explanation of world order, above all of the fact that what is, can be enjoyed by our contingent spirit, because it reflects God's goodness overflowing in a free act of creation. It is *through* such realization, however dim, of the superabundant sweetness of the divine, that the dark night of faith can suffuse our soul with its realization that God is love and that He makes us able to abide in His love. But faith's realization at once points us on to the value called chastity, *hagneia*, the sense of the holiness of the human body, because the body is the natural language of the human spirit and remains so when it is divinized through the faith that works by charity. Indeed, once divine charity has transformed any human individual, he as it were *has* to pass through the grave and gate of death to glorious resurrection. The cultural "future of belief," then, depends on how the Christian conscience ministers to urban man's self-confrontation by correctly placing the fact of our general bodily resurrection within the energy-field of our culture.

Weighed against such a destiny, any pleasure-seeking not ruled by conscience appears as a sort of sacrilege, a pitiable sign of alienation from God, our only true home. Just as they imply agnosticism, so too our promiscuity and our contraceptive and anovulant marital sexuality are often a symbolic condensation of pantheistic evolutionary theory in its modern ideological form. When men evacuate their minds of God and the invisible world of created spirit, material process in the form of an evolutionary world-picture crowds in to fill the vacuum. Now for such a world-picture, human generation is something men and women bring about, bringing sperm and ovum together to make a new man. But at this point our experience of our own self-knowledge, and thus of our own spirituality, gives the wise pause. Material forces cannot create spiritual joy, which is the need and destiny of man. In the eyes of historical mankind and of the Catholic Church there is something irreducibly mysterious about the fact that sexual congress can result in a new man, a new personality. Only God can make a man; He is not merely the remote ultimate author, He is necessarily, from the nature of the case, the *immediate* author, at least in part. Human fertilization forces His hand, just as a priest pronouncing the words of consecration does; but man and woman provide only the physical base; God alone can infuse personality, and God is thus the

immediate author of human history. The palaeonto-
logical mystery of human origins is renewed every
time a child is conceived. The generative act is awesome, seen in this light; it is, as the all-too-familiar
phrase has it, pro-creative, a sort of participation in
the divine act of creation. Consequently it is phrased
culturally as marriage, an act of conscience, a total life-
long consecration to generation, which was always,
for this reason, a sacrament.

Now it is faith's certitude and spiritual joy in turn
which make Christian chastity a light burden, and thus
liberate the body to become a language for the spirit.
The human body itself, as the supreme value in any
culture, is all-important in liberating conscience from
paralysis by doubt into religious consciousness. Men
falsely believing that the female body is an erotic object and that the male inseminating reflex is more or
less uncontrollable imagine that God's command to be
chaste is a command to fear the warmth of human
love and the familiar sight and touch of the body.
Nothing could be further from the truth. The whole
body is our word for ecstasy. The inspired word,
particularly in The Song of Songs, tells us that the gift
of God called chastity by Christians involves, in its
perfection, an uninhibited glorying in the human
body as the supreme beauty of this creation and the
link between this world and the world to come, the
new heaven and new earth. Read again, for instance,
the Song's praise of the bride, in the *Jerusalem Bible*:

How beautiful are your feet in their sandals,
O prince's daughter!
The curve of your thighs is like the curve of a necklace,
work of a master hand.
Your navel is a bowl well rounded
with no lack of wine,

your belly a heap of wheat
surrounded with lilies.
Your two breasts are two fawns,
twins of a gazelle.
Your neck is an ivory tower.
Your eyes, the pools of Heshbon,
by the gate of Bath-rabbim.
Your nose, the Tower of Lebanon,
sentinel facing Damascus.
Your head is held high like Carmel,
and its plaits are as dark as purple;
a king is held captive in your tresses.
How beautiful you are, how charming,
my love, my delight!
In stature like the palm tree,
its fruit-clusters your breasts.
"I will climb the palm tree," I resolved,
"I will seize its clusters of dates."
May your breasts be clusters of grapes,
your breath sweet-scented as apples,
your speaking, superlative wine.[9]

For this vision, faith's vision, there is no such thing as
a secular value. For the value behind all values in the
City of Man is the human body, the physical persons
we are, and we are not secular facts, we are sacred
facts. Here are words of prophecy, not made good till
the Blessed Virgin Mary, the Mother of our Saviour,
is assumed in glory of body as well as soul into heaven.
And what God has done in Mary is what He intends
for each one of us here.

Yet how can modern man, Darwin-Marx-Freud-
Einstein man, photographing Mars, come to faith's
vision of the human lot? They will not listen to Moses,
said Jesus; but neither will they listen to Gregory of
Nazianzen, nor to Thomas Aquinas, nor to Pius XII.
These are all old-fashioned, out-of-date; history is an

evolution; progress means that we do not need to listen to the dead. The dead? We too shall be among the dead soon enough. When men will not listen to other teachers, God always has one more teacher left to whom no man can refuse his ear: death, and all the suffering helplessness of mankind summed up in the word "death." In *The Waste Land*, between the sordeur of fornication and contraception and abortion, parts II and III, and the thunder's message of surrender and liberation and harmony, part V, lies the thought of death, part IV:

> Phlebas the Phoenician, a fortnight dead,
> Forgot the cry of gulls, and the deep sea swell
> And the profit and loss.[10]

Remember Phlebas, this lyric concludes, who was once handsome and tall as you. Death teaches the animal called man the most necessary of all his lessons: happiness cannot be allowed to be something we make or plan or imagine, for every thing that men plan or make or imagine is swept away by the flood of death, even the preaching of the Gospel and the saying of Mass. Lay not up your treasures upon earth, for moth and rust will eat them away and thieves will break in and steal—time and life, the greatest thieves of all, thieves of health, wealth, reputation, learning, power, pleasure. Yet what else is there? Is God a *reality* I can enjoy? Give me more time. I must have time to examine the question, to study all schools of thought, to read 1001 books by theological experts, and demythologize my thinking. "No!" insists Death: "Hasten. You have no time. The next sunrise may be *your* last. *Now* is the time for you to choose. *Now* is the only time any man can ever be happy, for the past is over and the future is not yet, and in any case will only be another now.

Our happiness must be possessed now, today. Take no
thought for the morrow. Let the dead past bury its
dead. Seek first the kingdom of God and His righteousness and the rest can look after itself." So death
readies us at last for the certitudes of the spiritual
order, delivering us from gossip, opinions, images,
wishful thinking, contemporary fashions, personal
routines, and bad habits. And so it was that physical
death was the language in which Christ Our Lord
chose to speak to all men. He speaks primarily by
dying. Our death can be joined to His and trans-
figured by it and open on to glorious resurrection.

When we examine how faith converts modern
doubt, we can see how some of the barriers are removed, by the quest for certitude and by serious
thinking about death. But in the final analysis, the
process we set out to describe is a mystery. I have
emphasized how important belief in the resurrection is.
Now not only is the resurrection itself a mystery of
Christianity, but the conviction of Christians concerning it, at all times and places, is also a mystery of
Christianity. Like every Christian mystery it is also a
fact, and for the untamed animal man a scandalous
fact, a fact that offends him mortally. The modern
mind has a huge store of hatred for men who come
telling it of the resurrection of the body and the life
of the world to come. All the more reason for being
scrupulously faithful in preaching it to them.

The notion of resurrection upsets the whole pose
of modernity in which our generation finds its only
deep comfort. The modern scientific world view, with
its evolutionary account of human origins, persuades
men to delete God, immortality, the permanent moral
law, from the list of questions at present answerable;
we are too busy synthesizing life in the laboratory,

solving the problem of death, establishing genetic con-
trols and seed-banks, to waste time on such ifs. The
doctrine of the resurrection ends such evasions and
equivocations and rhetoric about the marvellous dis-
coveries of science. Either it is so, or it is not so. If
you say it is not so, you have chosen against historical
Christianity and have no right to complain if your
choice fails to make you happy. If it is so, it puts an
end to the scientific dreamworlds. Among the resurrected, there must be one who was first, and first to
father others who would be resurrected, and him we
call Adam: no gradual ascent through the hominids,
so that Kenyapithecus is a little more resurrected than
Proconsul, but the First Man, in the abrupt glory of
his eternal destiny as a physical organism. And sexual
intercourse is no longer a means of filling time, but
the power to hand on that extraordinary destiny, a
daily miracle—a religious and awful thing—so that it
would quite literally be better to die than to be seriously wrong concerning its right use.

Only in the light of the resurrection does the
Christian scheme become real to modern man: one
Christ, who suffered for our salvation, descended into
Hades, rose again from the dead, ascended into heaven,
sat down at the right hand of the Father: whence He
shall come to judge the quick and the dead. At whose
coming all men shall rise again with their bodies: and
shall give account for their own deeds. And they that
have done good will go into life eternal; they that have
done evil into eternal fire. This is the Catholic faith:
which except a man do faithfully and steadfastly
believe, he cannot be saved.[11] When we say, in this
ancient credal statement, that a man must believe the
Catholic faith to be saved—a position repeated by the
bishops at Vatican II—we do not mean, believe in so

many words. It is not with words that we believe. It is with our whole suffering, living, and dying flesh. It is better to be silent and to be than to speak and not to be.

II

Faith full-grown knows a peace which overwhelms understanding. And this peace, like faith its root, cannot be understood from the outside, and is not the product of ordinary analytical acts of understanding, the way the conclusions of physics, psychoanalysis, or historical investigation are. If you should ask how this enjoyment of faith's mysteries comes about, it is a matter of grace rather than of the process of teaching; of desire rather than the pursuit of study; the spouse of the soul rather than the words of the *magisterium*; it is a work of God rather than man; it is darkness rather than light. But let us speak of a consuming fire which engulfs us in God, the fire which is God. We choose death and pass over into darkness when we know this wisdom; we impose silence on all the anxieties of historical existence, on all the images of fancy, on all desire for anything other than God, who spoke from the burning bush to Moses, saying: "I am who am. Say He Who Is sent you to them." [12]

This is the darkness of profound conversion, where we turn to God as He turns to us. On the one hand, our understanding grows up towards the judgment wherein it understands that there are some things it cannot understand. On the other hand, God pours in the deep but dazzling darkness of faith *through* the light of that judgment, and indeed, in practice, we only reach that judgment which marks the ultimate limit of our power of understanding *because* God has poured in His light of revelation as faith, a great sea bathing the individual mind in every one of its thoughts. Slowly the heart comes to realize that its concept of person contains depths of meaning beyond its natural grasp. God is more unlike anything we mean by person than He is like what we mean by it; but still it remains true to say that it is only through the concept of person-to-person love, or friendship as we call it, that Faith can understand God at all. Divine personality is more unlike than like human personality; yet so open is human nature on the divine, so capable of it, that God Himself can be a fully human person.

Our two-fold conversion therefore involves a two-fold process in the human understanding. God's initiative, giving the light of faith, is everything. But our analytical understanding has a natural aptitude for this gift of light, and consequently makes a strong, active response to its presence in the heart. So that both preceding and following the gift of faith there is a purification of our philosophical, scientific, and historical investigations to the point at which our minds can open up to and enjoy such truths as the resurrection of the man Jesus, His presence in the bread and wine, the gift of infallibility in the Church of His elect, and our power to pray and suffer and merit on behalf of one another. At the same time we learn to see and avoid errors. The gravest obstacle to our supernatural growth in faith turns out to be the false dogmas which our culture seeks to impose on us. Instances are the conviction that miracles do not happen or that transubstantiation is a medieval conception and now out of date; or the notion that the Gospels are human documents, the work of undisciplined minds and heated imaginations, whereas in truth they were the work of men perpetually in the presence of the divine mystery, who were thus preserved, by purity of conscience, from error; or again the modern illusion that psychoanalysis, group therapy, group dynamics and the like are the chief way to liberate our personalities rather than prayer, the study of sacred theology, self-denial, and the study of the lives of the saints. Without being able to solve every difficulty, answer every question, we see through such culture-dogmas; we see their arbitrary character, and see, consequently, how an opposite way of thinking is possible and indeed necessary if we are to be sane human beings. Sanity is not conformity to our society, for our society may be insane; sanity is conformity to the real. We are not ready for God's intimate friendship until we have got rid of every false idea.

This active purification of the human understanding, opening on the world of divine beauty, was expounded in pagan antiquity by Plato. The words of Diotima to Socrates in the *Symposium* are not only classical Greece's highest moment, they are perhaps the noblest moment of world literature outside of Christianity. Because of their irreplaceable importance, permit me to quote them at sufficient length:

"These are the lesser mysteries of love, into which even you, Socrates, may enter; I do not know if you will be able to attain the greater and more advanced ones which are the final cause of these, if they are rightly pursued. But I will do my utmost to inform you, and do you follow if you can. He who wishes to approach love rightly should turn in youth to beautiful forms, and first love one such form only—out of that he should create fair thoughts; and soon he will of himself perceive that the beauty of one form is akin to the beauty of another; and then if beauty of form in general is his pursuit, how foolish would he be not to recognize that the beauty in every form is one and the same! And when he perceives this he will cease to concentrate his love on a single object—that will seem foolish and petty to him—and will become a lover of all beautiful forms; in the next stage he will consider that the beauty of the mind is more honourable than the beauty of the outward form. So that if he meets someone with few charms of person but whose nature is beautiful, he will be content to love and care for him, and will bring to birth thoughts which make youth better, until he is compelled to contemplate and see the beauty of institutions and laws, and to understand that the beauty of them all is akin, and that personal beauty is a trifle; and after laws and institutions he will go on to the sciences, that he may see their beauty, and not be like a servant in love with the beauty of one youth or man or institution, slavish, mean, and petty, but drawing towards and contemplating the vast sea of beauty, he will create many fair and lofty thoughts and notions in boundless love of wisdom; until on that shore he grows great and strong, and at last the vision is revealed to him of a single science, which is the science of beauty everywhere. And now try, she said, to give me all your mind.

"He who has been instructed so far in the mystery of love, and who has learned to see the beautiful correctly and in due order, when he comes toward the end will suddenly perceive a wondrous beauty (and this, Socrates, is the final cause of all our former toils). It is eternal, uncreated, indestructible, subject neither to increase or decay; not like other things partly beautiful, partly ugly; not beautiful at one time or in one relation or in one place, and deformed in other times, other relations, other places; not beautiful in the opinion of some and ugly in the opinion of others. It is not to be imagined as a beautiful face or form or any part of the body, or in the likeness of speech or knowledge; it does not have its being in any living thing or in the sky or the earth or any other place. It is Beauty absolute, separate, simple, and everlasting, which without diminution, and without increase, or any change, is imparted to the ever-growing and perishing beauties of all other things. If a man ascends from these under the influence of the right love of a friend, and begins to perceive that beauty, he may reach his goal. And the true order of approaching the mystery of love is to begin from the beauties of earth and mount upwards for the sake of that other beauty, using these as steps only, and from one going on to two, and from two to all beautiful forms, and from beautiful forms to beauty of conduct, and from beauty of conduct to beauty of knowledge, until from this we arrive at the knowledge of absolute beauty, and at last know what the essence of beauty is. This, my dear Socrates," said the stranger of Mantineia, "is the life above all others which man should live, in the contemplation of beauty absolute; a beauty which if you once beheld, you would see not to be after the measure of gold, and dress, and fair boys and youths, whose sight now entrances you. . . . But what if man had eyes to see the true beauty—the divine beauty, I mean, pure and clear and unalloyed, not clogged with pollutions of mortality and all the colours and vanities of human life—gazing on it, in communion with the true beauty simple and divine? Remember how in that communion only, beholding beauty with the eye of the mind, he will be able to bring forth, not shadows of beauty, but its truth, because it is no shadow that he grasps, but the truth; and he will give birth to true virtue and nourish it and become the friend of God and be immortal as far as mortal man may. Would that be an ignoble life?"

Such, Phaedrus, were the words of Diotima; and I am convinced of their truth.[13]

Now there is no human understanding altogether incapable of feeling the attraction of this intellectual adventure, the pull of the thought of God. The mightiest of the modern atheistic thinkers, Marx, Engels, Nietzsche, Freud, knew this moment only too well, desperately fighting its attractions as a trap for man, a siren song enticing him away from his proper hap-

piness in this world. If they succeeded among the
literate, it is because the Idea of the Good lacks ex-
planatory power in relation to the real physical world
in which we are immersed. But if they succeeded
among the masses, it is simply because for most men
God is little more than a passing thought—if that. It
is too high, too rare an atmosphere for their restless,
greedy, probing analytical powers; men cannot rest
there, cannot long feel at home there. Besides, the way
is steep, sharp, rugged, too hard and dry and painful
for flesh and blood, a veritable ascent of Mount
Carmel. Plato has also described for us the pain of this
intellectual awakening to the invisible world by his
famous metaphor of the cave in the *Republic*. Plato
describes a group of captives chained so that they can
see nothing but shadows cast on the wall of their cave
by passing figures. Such, he suggests, is the position of
the human understanding as it engages with the invisible world.

And now look again, and see what will naturally follow
if the prisoners are released and disabused of their error.
At first, when any of them is liberated and compelled
suddenly to stand up and turn his neck and walk and look
towards the light, he will suffer sharp pains; the glare
will distress him, and he will be unable to see the realities
of which in his former state he had seen the shadows; and
then conceive some one saying to him, that what he saw
before was an illusion, but that now, when he is approaching nearer to reality and his eye is turned towards more
real existence, he has a clearer vision—what will be his
reply? And you may further imagine that his instructor
is pointing to the objects as they pass and requiring him
to name them—will he not be perplexed? Will he not
fancy that the shadows which he previously saw are truer
than the objects which are now shown to him? And if
he is compelled to look straight at the light, will he not

have a pain in his eyes which will make him turn away to the shadows which he can see, and which he will conceive to be in reality clearer than the things which are now being shown to him? And suppose once more, that he is reluctantly dragged up a steep and rugged ascent, and not released until he is forced into the presence of the sun itself, is he not likely to be hurt and annoyed? When he approaches the light his eyes will be dazzled, and he will not be able to see anything at all of what are now called realities. He will have to grow accustomed to the sight of the upper world.[14]

"He will have to grow accustomed to the sight of the upper world." This passive purification of the understanding to the point at which it becomes accustomed to the upper world is what we chiefly mean by the word *conversion*. The law of the Lord is unspotted, converting souls; the commandment of the Lord is lightsome, enlightening the eyes. Our religious tradition is, always has been, and always will be, a tradition sustained by *converts*. The convert is a man who never loses his sense of wonder at what God has done in him. And there has always been tension and hostility between this tradition and the main body of contemporary culture—between the Church and the modern world (for the world always thought itself modern)—because the Church always demanded of the world this same one thing that has happened to it: conversion, metanoia, repentance. Abraham, a middle-class Babylonian, is *called from* his modern city and his class, Moses is *called from* the court life of Egypt, Amos is *called from* his herds, Matthew from his tax-bench, Peter from his nets, Saul from his false ideology. Again and again it happens. Who could have been more typical of the permissive society of the decaying Roman Empire than Augustine?

For this space of nine years then (from my nineteenth year, to my eight and twentieth) we lived seduced and seducing, deceived and deceiving, in divers lusts . . . , hunting after the emptiness of popular praise . . . , the follies of shows, and the intemperance of desires.[15]

Wretched I was; and wretched is every soul bound by the friendship of perishable things; he is torn asunder when he loses them, and then he feels the wretchedness which he had ere he lost them,[16]

loathing to live, fearing to die. Again, who could have been more typical of the medieval bourgeoisie than Francis of Assisi, or of the Renaissance nobility of Europe than Ignatius of Loyola?

But there are immense differences between their accounts of conversion and that of Plato. Plato's God is a passive Thing, an Idea, waiting for us, in our good time, according as we feel inclined, to gaze upon its beauty. The God of Abraham and Moses is a living and active God, impatient, a person at once terrible and merciful. And we know we have sinned against Him. We have said not only how Christ's resurrection is a mystery of faith, but how our faith, too, is a mystery of faith. Now let us say also that sin and God's permission of sin is a mystery impenetrable to understanding, something we simply accept, leaving us aghast at God's greatest mystery, His inward transformation of human sinners into His intimate friends. Those who use Loyola's prayer are perhaps through custom inclined to miss the sheer naked passion it displays, a sort of shock at the unexpectedness of God's mercy: Soul of Christ, sanctify me. Body of Christ, save me. Blood of Christ, inebriate me. Water from the side of Christ, wash me. Passion of Christ, strengthen me. O good Jesus, hear me, hear me. It is true that perfect love casts out fear. But that is true only when we stand safe on the summit of the mountain. All the way up, clinging desperately to the side of the sheer cliff with a many-thousand-foot drop below us, love and fear intermingle and interpenetrate. They both draw their thrust and fierceness from the same source: our knowledge that God has no need of us but that we have an infinite need of God. So there is a dialectic of fear and love, where the greatness of our desire for God makes our fear of losing Him great, and our fear of losing Him makes our love ever harder, more pure, more ruthless. For this love is as harsh as Hades, and is the only thing that is as harsh as Hades. W. H. Auden's account of this dialectic of love and fear is presumably an account of his own turning towards Christianity:

> Descend into the fosse of Tribulation,
> Take the cold hand of Terror for a guide;
> Below you in its swirling desolation
> Hear tortured Horror roaring for a bride:
> O do not falter at the last request
> But, as the huge deformed head rears to kill,
> Answer its craving with a clear I Will;
> Then wake, a child in the rose-garden, pressed
> Happy and sobbing to your lover's breast.[17]

We must descend into the fosse of tribulation before we can wake like a child in the rose garden. Alphonsus of Ligouri's *Way of Salvation* remorselessly insists on those austere and frightening meditations which change proud self-sufficient spirits into open and teachable men and women, and transform lax and mediocre Catholics into people aflame with love of God—the frequent thought of death; the unhappy life of the sinner; the journey to eternity; the blindness of those who say: if we be lost we shall not be lost alone; the evil of lukewarmness; the rashness of sinners in

committing mortal sin; giving ourselves over to God
without reserve; trouble and confusion at the hour of
death; provoking God by sin to depart from us; the
abuse of grace.

Now the classical analysis of the mystery of sin,
which nevertheless respects and preserves the beauty
and thrust of Plato's upward ascent, is the *Confessions*
of Augustine.

Having then read those books of the Platonists, and thence
been taught to search for incorporeal truth, I saw Thy
invisible things, understood by those things which are
made . . . ; of these things I was assured, yet too unsure
to enjoy Thee. . . . I did not weep, but was puffed up
with my knowledge. For where was that charity building
upon the foundation of humility, which is Christ Jesus?
. . . Upon these, I believe, Thou willedst that I should
fall, before I studied Thy Scriptures, that it might be im-
printed on my memory, how I was affected by them;
and that afterwards when my spirits were tamed through
Thy books, and my wounds touched by Thy healing
fingers, I might discern and distinguish between presump-
tion and confession; between those who saw whither they
were to go, yet saw not the way, that way which leads us
not only to behold but to dwell in the beatific country.[18]

"The true order of approaching the mystery of love,"
as Plato said, "is to begin from the beauties of earth
and mount upwards for the sake of that other beauty,
using these as steps only." Why does this lovely ascent
not happen? Why is the height not held once reached?
When we say that *sin* is the answer, we give, as I said,
a very mysterious answer, for sin is a non-thing, a
failure to keep moving upwards to our true and only
happiness. Instead of the momentum of our thrust
forward, we stop on the step, as though anything else
can compare with the power to gaze on God as a

friend. And the absurd thing about this (for sin alone
is the real existential absurdity) is, as Augustine shows
in many places, that the sinner is pretending to himself, and the knowledge that he is pretending, play-
acting, is itself punishment enough of his sin.

Each man's own sin is the instrument of his punishment,
and his iniquity is turned into his torment; that we may
not think, that that serenity and ineffable light of God
need produce out of itself that whereby sins were to be
punished; for He so disposeth sins, that what were delights
to men sinning, are the instruments of the Lord punish-
ing.[19]

The sinner claims to have what God alone has, and is
punished by his knowledge of the emptiness of his
claim:

Pride imitates exaltedness; whereas Thou alone art God
exalted over all. Ambition, what seeks it, but honours and
glory? whereas Thou alone art to be honoured above
all, and glorious for evermore. The cruelty of the great
would fain be feared; but who is to be feared but God
alone, out of whose power what can be wrested or with-
drawn? The tenderness of the wanton would fain be
counted love: yet is nothing more tender than Thy
charity; nor is aught loved more healthfully than Thy
truth, bright and beautiful above all. Curiosity makes
semblance of a desire of knowledge; whereas Thou su-
premely knowest all. Yes, sloth would fain be at rest; but
Thou art the fulness and never-failing plenteousness of
incorruptible pleasures. Prodigality presents a shadow of
liberality: but Thou art the most overflowing Giver of
all good. Covetousness would possess many things: and
Thou possessest all things. Envy disputes for excellency:
what more excellent than Thou?
    Thus doth the soul commit fornication, when she turns
from Thee, seeking without Thee what she findeth not

pure and untainted, till she returns to Thee. Thus all
pervertedly imitate Thee, who remove far from Thee,
and lift themselves up against Thee. But even by thus
imitating Thee, they imply Thee to be the Creator of
all nature; whence there is not place whither altogether
to retire from Thee.[20]

Thus God overcomes sin in us by being more *pleasur-
able* than any sin can be. He pleaseth God whom
God pleaseth. And this pleasure in God is very particularly a pleasure in the sheer power of God: I
believe in God the Father almighty. Why do we say
"almighty" rather than "all-wise" or "most beautiful"? It is because the mind that can say "I believe"
has seen God's mightiest work, breaking down the
pretenses behind which sinful man barricades himself
against God's awful holiness. No man can be certain
of religious truth, says the modern world. But God
has the power to make a modern man truly certain
concerning the hidden nature of God and His provi-
dence over every human life. Lord, we say, you remain remote, unreal, compared with supermarkets,
movies, sexual intercourse, and getting drunk. No,
He replies, I have the power to transform you into
My lover, so that you say, "I to my Beloved, and my
Beloved to me, till the day break and the shadows
retire." God has the *power* to become a man who rose
from the dead and reigns glorious forever; the *power*
to create a church whose unity, doctrine and fruitful-
ness do not fail; the *power* to convert sinners; the
power to purify the souls of the dead and restore them
to bodily life. The theories of philosophers and theologians, no matter how contemporary, cannot take
away the power of God to do what He wills. Above
all we know that if God commands a thing, He gives
it. To know that He commands chastity is to know

that He gives chastity, and the same holds good for religious unity, full employment, missionary zeal, international cooperation, and the rest.

God's commandment, however, is not this or that virtue in isolation, but the balance, the whole system of the virtues, and we call it conversion only when justice is tempered with mercy, prudence vitalized by bold creativity, purity accompanied by human warmth and openness, and large-minded courage by humility. Only when faith grows towards understanding and charity towards a wisdom that disposes all things strongly and sweetly from end to end, only then do we have religious conversion. And conversion, conversion alone, is capable of that total, comprehensive and systematic body of knowledge, that understanding of the world in terms of its ultimate explanation, which we call wisdom, theology, synthesis, Catholicism. Wisdom presupposes conversion—that is, it presupposes horror of sin and doctrinal error; it is precisely the claim to wisdom, or synthesis, without horror of sin, that constitutes that philosophy and vain deceit which the Apostle Paul warns against. But at the same time, synthesis or wisdom is the test of true conversion. This is the great theme of the inspired Scripture which we call The Book of Wisdom: "Into a soul that plots evil wisdom enters not, nor dwells she in a body under debt of sin";[21] "The love of God is honorable wisdom," and that wisdom, which "teaches temperance and prudence, justice and fortitude,"[22] and so "produces friends of God and prophets,"[23] at the same time gives "sound knowledge of existing things, that I might know the organization of the universe."[24]

Now let us not play-act; let us not pretend that these classical moments, which I have culled from

Plato and the scriptures, Augustine and Loyola, cease to hold for modern man. The only thing that has changed is the disguise worn by the enemy. Now he wears the theory of evolution, or the theory that human history so conditions human consciousness that the individual mind cannot transcend history and by faith grasp the things of eternity even while living in this world of time. Or he appears as the great modern dogma that no one can be sure, absolutely sure, beyond the shadow of a doubt, about such things as God, the divinity of Jesus Christ, purgatory, hell, or the need for chastity. Our behaviour shows how we are seduced from the love of God by two particular distractions above all others, the vast intricacy of our technology and organization, and (by way of reaction against this) the cult of sexual fulfilment. Both, of course, are subtle forms of egotism. Yet individuals continually, in fact, overcome all cultural obstacles. English literature, from Bunyan's *Grace Abounding* and Herbert's *Temple*, is peculiarly rich in accounts of conversion. In the twentieth century, the century of Marx, Freud, and Einstein, we have classical instances of conversion from the modern post-Christian culture-complex to a firm, dogmatic, and ascetical Christianity in the works of poets such as T. S. Eliot, W. H. Auden, and Edith Sitwell, and of prose writers such as G. K. Chesterton, C. S. Lewis, Thomas Merton, and Karl Stern. There are, of course, many outside the English heritage, such as Sigrid Undset, Jacques Maritain, John Wu, and Boris Pasternak. And the greatest of all modern accounts, by far, is Kierkegaard's *Sickness Unto Death,* an analysis sketched out in more accessible form in his discourse entitled: *Man's Need of God Constitutes his Highest Perfection.*

Sometimes, as in Hopkins's *The Wreck of the Deutschland*, the account of conversion is very personal:

Thou knowest the walls, altar and hour and night:
The swoon of a heart that the sweep and the hurl of
      thee trod
Hard down with a horror of height:
And the midriff astrain with leaning of, laced with fire
      of stress.[25]

But more often it is universalized. T. S. Eliot's

> . . . There was a Birth, certainly,
> We had evidence and no doubt . . .[26]

is in the same tradition as Dryden's

> Dim as the borrow'd beams of Moon and Stars
> To lonely, weary, wand'ring Travellers
> Is reason to the soul.[27]

Francis Thompson's

> Thou dravest love from thee who dravest Me[28]

is in the same tradition as Dr. Johnson's *Vanity of Human Wishes*. All draw their conversion from one premise: that man's need of God constitutes his highest perfection. What is most intimate in each, his need of God, is what he shares most completely with every other human being. That is why the convert is always, from the nature of the case, an apostle. Conversion and apostolate alike must proceed from wrestling with what is basic and unavoidable and elementary and primitive, and that is why it clings to the simplest language, of birth and death, of light and darkness, of friendship and war, of sex and the seasons—and of resurrection. There is no expression for conversion

that can compare with Jesus's physical resurrection—
and our own, and the physical link between these, the
Eucharistic banquet where Christ's Body vitalizes ours.
When the unborn God in the human heart knows for
a moment all sublimities, it speaks the universal language of the bread, as Edith Sitwell says in one of her
poems, and gold-bearded thunders and hierarchies of
heaven roar from the earth: "Our Christ is arisen, He
comes to give a sign from the Dead."

The simplest of language, this: *homo homini res
sacra, gloria Dei vivens homo*. The body is the only
language natural to man, the one indestructibly sacred
language. Consequently the corruption of human sexuality is the most powerful symbol that we have of
human corruption, of original sin; and the conversion
of the sexual sinner the most vivid symbol that we
have of the meaning of conversion. This is the meaning of Pasternak's *Zhivago* poems on Mary Magdalene.
Her words are the words of every sinner:

> With nightfall my familiar comes,
> The reckoning I owe my past,
> And then my heart is gnawed within
> By recollections of my lust,
> The days when I was prey to men,
> A fool senseless and indiscreet
> Whose only haunt was in the street.

Her penitence, her fearful confession of helplessness,
is every sinner's sorrow:

> And just a few moments remain—
> Then comes the silence of the tomb.
> But now before the minutes take
> Me, here upon the final brink,
> My life before you I would break,
> An alabaster vase of doom.

Her turning to a new life, strangely continuous with the old even in its abruptest discontinuity, is every sinner's conversion:

> For, oh, my teacher and my Saviour,
> Just where and what now would I be
> Did not waiting eternity
> Approach my table each nightfall
> As though another client fell
> Into the meshes of my guile?
>
> But tell me simply what sin means,—
> What death, and hell, and brimstone flame?—
> When I, as everyone can see,
> In boundless sorrow one and same
> Grow into you, graft on a tree;

Yes, indeed: it is always because my yearning is beyond all measure; because I need God more than I need all other things, possible or actual, together; because my need of God constitutes my only perfection —this is why conversion comes to me, to each. We embrace Jesus's feet, His Church:

> And, Jesus, when I hold you fast,
> Your feet upon my bending knees,
> Perhaps I'm learning to embrace
> The rough cross with its four-square beam,
> And swoon to strain your body close
> And to prepare you for the tomb.[29]

Such, says Pasternak, in effect, is the meaning of the Russian Revolution. But the spirit of revolution, both then and now, both there and here, is the deadliest enemy of God's revolution—the revolution of the Spirit.

NOTES

1. Eph. 4:17–19.
2. T. S. Eliot, *The Waste Land*, in *Collected Poems of T. S. Eliot 1909–1962* (New York: Harcourt, Brace & World, 1963, and London: Faber & Faber), lines 37–41. Reprinted by permission.
3. *Ibid.*, lines 147–152, 156–159.
4. *Ibid.*, lines 403–405.
5. *Ibid.*, lines 411–413.
6. *Ibid.*, lines 417–422.
7. J. H. Newman, "The Infidelity of the Future," in *Catholic Sermons of Cardinal Newman* (London, 1957), p. 118, and *Grammar of Assent*, edited by E. Gilson (New York: Image Books, 1955), p. 180.
8. *The City of God*, 19,18, translated by John Healey (London: Dent, 1950).
9. Song of Songs in the *Jerusalem Bible* translation (New York: Doubleday, 1966), 7:2ff.
10. *The Waste Land*, lines 312–314.
11. The Athanasian Symbol from the Anglican *Book of Common Prayer*.
12. Cf. Bonaventure, *The Mind's Road to God*, translated by George Boas (Indianapolis: Bobbs-Merrill, 1953), Ch. V, pp. 34–38, Ch. VII, pp. 43–46.
13. Plato, *Symposium*, 202ff., in *Plato, Selected Passages*, edited by R. W. Livingstone (London: Oxford University Press, 1948), pp. 69–71.
14. Plato, *Republic*, 514ff., in *op. cit.*, pp. 49–50.
15. *The Confessions of St. Augustine*, 4, 1, translated by E. B. Pusey (London: Dent, 1945).
16. *Ibid.*, 4, 6.
17. W. H. Auden, "A Christmas Oratorio," in *For the Time Being* (New York: Random House, 1946). Reprinted by permission.
18. *Confessions*, 7, 20.
19. *In Ps.*, 7, 15.
20. *Confessions*, 2, 6.
21. Wisdom 1:4.
22. Wisdom 8:7.
23. Wisdom 7:27.
24. Wisdom 7:17.
25. Gerard Manley Hopkins, *The Wreck of the Deutschland*,

in *Poems of Gerard Manley Hopkins*, third edition (London: Oxford University Press, 1949), p. 56.

26. T. S. Eliot, *Journey of the Magi*, lines 36–37, in *op. cit.*

27. John Dryden, *Religio Laici* in *The Poems of John Dryden*, edited by John Sargeaunt (London: Oxford University Press, 1913), p. 99.

28. Francis Thompson, *The Hound of Heaven*, in *Modern American Poetry, Modern British Poetry*, edited by Louis Untermeyer (New York: Harcourt, Brace, 1950), p. 90.

29. "Mary Magdalen" from "The Poems of Yury Zhivago," in Boris Pasternak, *In the Interlude: Poems, 1945–1960*, translated by Henry Kamen (London: Oxford University Press, 1962), p. 46; a retranslation of the poetry in Boris Pasternak, *Doctor Zhivago*, translated by Max Hayward and Manya Harari (New York: Pantheon, 1959). Reprinted by permission of A. D. Peters & Co.